Early Learning Environments that Work

Rebecca Isbell and Betty Exelby

Illustrations: Garry Exelby

Photographs: Mike Talley, Susan Lachmann, and Su Lorencen

Dedications

To my mother,

who helped me appreciate beautiful things in my environment.
To my father,

who taught me how to "take pictures" in my mind.
I will cherish those visual images forever.

—Rebecca Isbell

To Mom,

who laid the foundation for a joyful and life-long romp with
colour and design.
To Dad,

who introduced me to the wonders of construction and how to
build spaces for living.

—Betty Exelby

Acknowledgements

We want to extend special thanks to Gary Exelby, the artist who has so effectively interpreted our many ideas into visual representations. The wonderful illustrations help us to see the possibilities that are open to us as we begin to change our environments. His creative work has added much to the design and effectiveness of our book.

Our grateful appreciation is given to Sheila Smith, who provided technical assistance on the manuscript. She has pleasantly re-read the words and made the many changes necessary to make the text flow smoothly.

Mike Talley is the photographer who captured the wonderful moments of young children participating in a meaningful environment. His willingness to spend the time necessary to photograph these special happenings is greatly appreciated. Susan Lachmann and Su Lorencen also contributed several very special photographs.

The photographs were taken in the Infant Toddler Program and Child Study Center. These programs are a part of the Center of Excellence in Early Childhood Learning and Development located on the East Tennessee State University Campus in Johnson City, Tennessee.

early learning
Environments
THAT WORK

Rebecca Isbell and Betty Exelby

gryphon house, inc.
Silver Spring, MD

Published by Gryphon House, Inc.

10770 Columbia Pike, Suite 201, Silver Spring, MD 20901

Visit us on the web at www.gryphonhouse.com

Illustrations: Garry Exelby

Cover illustration: Joan Waites

Reprinted April 2010

Library of congress Cataloging-in-Publication Data

Isbell, Rebecca,

    Early learning environments that work / Rebecca Isbell and Betty Exelby; illustrations, Gary Exelby; photographs, Mike Talley, Susan Lachmann, an Su Lorencen.

        p. cm.

    Includes bibliographical refernces and index.

    ISBN 978-0-87659-256-4

    1. Early childhood education—Planning. 2. Classroom environment—Psychological aspects. 3. Day care centers—Design and construction. I. Exelby, Betty, Date II. Title.

LB1139.23 .I72 2001

372.21—dc21

                          2001023162

Bulk purchase

Gryphon House books are available at special discount when purchased in bulk for special premiums and sales promotions as well as for fund-raising use. Special editions or book excerpts also can be created to specification. For details, contact the Director of Sales at Gryphon House.

Disclaimer

The publisher and the authors cannot be held responsible for injury, mishap, or damages incurred during the use of or because of the information in this book. The authors recommend appropriate and reasonable supervision at all times based on the age and capability of each child.

Table of Contents

Chapter 5—Aspects of Quality Environments for Children

Chapter 6—Assessing What You Have

Chapter 9—Enriching the Environment

Chapter 10—Extending Your Understanding

References 123

Appendices

Index 177

Preface

Five years ago, Betty and I met on a study tour of the early childhood programs in Reggio Emilia, Italy. Both of us had been working with early childhood programs for many years and had been teaching courses related to environments for young children. Although we had been studying and creating environments for young children, we were amazed at the incredible spaces that the Italians had designed for them, and we were inspired by the beautiful places we saw for young children in their schools. We were impressed with their view of the capabilities of young children, and we marveled at the collaborations of teachers and parents. We wanted to share the special places that we saw in Italy with early childhood teachers in the United States and Canada. We realized that most of our early childhood teachers would never have the opportunity to see these beautiful classrooms in Italy.

So, we began the mission of sharing with teachers the possibilities for designing wonderful, aesthetically pleasing spaces for young children that had inspired us to think in new ways. Each of us brings to our writing unique experiences that color (colour) our interpretation of the Reggio Emilia program. We have lived and worked our entire lives in North America. But we believe that our cultural experiences in the United States and Canada provide a background for a unique interpretation of the Reggio Emilia environment. In this book, we have set out to help early childhood teachers recognize the importance of the environment and to provide practical tools they can use to design beautiful, meaningful places for both children and themselves. It is our wish that children in our countries will be able to experience wonderful environments as inspired as those we saw in Italy.

A Note From the Authors

As Betty and I worked together, we began to realize that some of the words that we were using were both spelled and pronounced differently in our two countries (for example, color and colour). In addition, some of the words that we used to identify the same thing were completely different (for example, cabinet and cupboard). Since we wanted to respect the language of both our regions, we have included both the United States and the Canadian spelling the first time one of these words is used in each chapter. Our collaboration has demonstrated to us that although we may say it in different ways we share the common belief that we want beautiful places for young children and their teachers.

Glossary of United States or Canadian Words

Behavior (behaviour)

Cabinet (cupboard)

Catalog (catalogue)

Center (centre)

Color (colour)

Favorite (favourite)

Meter (metre)

Switch (toggle)

Theater (theatre)

A CHALLENGING PUZZLE:

FLOOR PLANS

FIXED FEATURES - doors, windows, walls, celings

AESTHETICS

TOOLS and MATERIALS

BUDGET

CHILDREN'S ZONES of ACTIVITY

PARENT and TEACHER SPACES

STORAGE

CREATIVITY

DISPLAY

REGULATION GUIDELINES

COLOUR

DECORATING with ACCESSORIES

PLANTS

SPACE

TEACHER'S DESIGN EXPERIENCES

DESIGNING CHILDREN'S ENVIRONMENTS

chapter 1

The Power of the Environment and Its Impact on Children

Young children strive to understand the world in which they live. They try to understand the visual images and concrete objects in their environment. Through the unique and concrete experiences that children have as they interact with their environment, they learn how the world works. The environment in which this learning takes place can enrich and expand the quality of children's experiences. Therefore, children, teachers, and parents must work together and use their resources in the most effective way.

Today's Children

Many of today's young children are spending a large number of hours in a "new" environment—childcare. Children who enter childcare as infants can spend as many as 12,000 hours there before they enter school. It is, therefore, essential to examine the environment carefully to determine how to create the best place for young children. Children learn by exploring and investigating, so their environment should support and encourage this. The environment must be attractive, exciting, and a place where children can work and play using appropriate resources, materials, and tools.

4-year-old in large motor play

The Goals of This Book

This book will examine the childcare environment with the vision of making it a place where young children will be physically, emotionally, aesthetically, and intellectually nurtured. The primary task of this book is to help teachers explore the possibilities of the physical environment of the classroom so that children in their care will develop to their maximum intellectual and emotional potential.

Included in this book are practical ways for teachers to design enriched environments that will encourage children to actively participate according to their special ways of learning. The design principles explored in this book will help teachers develop an effective classroom that provides children with settings for a variety of types of experiences, including active and quiet play and individual and small group activities.

This book focuses on how to create an appropriate, practical, and interesting place for learning. Teachers will learn how to create a beautiful and meaningful classroom, filled with real experiences and natural materials. The authors have selected the examples in this book to spark your imagination and challenge your creative spirit. Interwoven throughout the book are multitudes of practical options to help you generate ideas for changing the environment.

Questions to Be Examined in This Book

1. How can you design a classroom environment to have a positive influence on the development of young children?

2. How can a classroom provide both a stimulating learning environment and a calm, safe place?
3. How do you select and organize equipment, furnishings, and materials so young children can make choices and focus on their work?
4. Can you develop a plan to enhance the environment in small, manageable steps?
5. How can you implement an environmental design using low-cost and readily accessible materials?
6. Can principles of design be used to create a nurturing environment for young children, their parents, and their teachers?
7. How will these experiences in developing environmental space impact and extend the professional growth of the classroom teacher?

You can apply the basic information and practical tools for creating a beautiful early childhood classroom that supports learning to multiple rooms or to an entire school. The information in this book will provide a strategy to plan and implement an organized and meaningful place where children and adults can live together in harmony. The photographs and illustrations provide the stimulus for discussion and collaboration between all who use the space—children and adults—as the environment becomes a new focus of attention and enhancement.

A Caring, Knowledgeable Teacher: A Critical Component

Research has clearly indicated that a trained and caring teacher is the most critical element in a quality early childhood classroom. When a knowledgeable and caring teacher uses the design techniques included in this book, he or she can make the environment a wonderful place for nurturing the development of young children. The teacher can provide children with many opportunities to expand their knowledge by actively participating in an environment that is appropriate for their level of development. Children will come to understand how their world works as they grow and interact within this effectively designed space.

An Environment That Matches Young Children

The first step in creating an appropriate environment for infants, toddlers, and young children is to examine how children develop. Each age has unique characteristics that correspond to a particular stage of development, which varies by individual. How children interact with the environment and each other should influence the room arrangement, available materials, and what happens within the space.

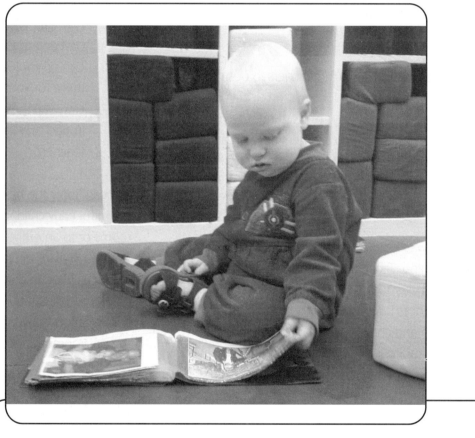

Toddler "reading" personal book

Infants and Toddlers

Infant in ball-play

Infants and toddlers learn about their world by manipulating objects and materials. As a toddler feels the texture of a beach ball while pushing and rolling it across the floor, he constructs his understanding of the ball. Since very young children learn in this manner, it is essential to design an environment that allows them many opportunities to explore real materials.

Infants and toddlers learn about people through their interactions with them. Caring people encourage infant and toddlers' social/emotional development. Children will believe they are capable learners if people respond to them and support their growing curiosity. They discover their developing abilities as they interact with people and materials in meaningful ways.

During this period of development, language begins as toddlers try to find "labels" for all the objects and people in their world. Language gives them new power to question and find answers. A frequent question asked by toddlers is, "What's that?" These new labels provide children with a basis for language development and the foundation for future language expansion.

Interactive play between toddler and teacher

Preschoolers' Development

Preschoolers are active learners who are growing and learning in many different ways. They constantly examine and experiment with their physical and social world, and they develop symbolic representations as they participate in socio-dramatic play. Construction materials, such as blocks and boxes, become increasingly important to children as they use them to represent their concrete experiences. In addition, they begin to cooperate as they work and play together.

During this period of development, preschoolers are curious and interested in learning about their world, and they have many creative ideas and approaches. They are capable of making decisions and choices, selecting materials to implement projects, and determining desired learning centers (centres) and play themes. And, they are able to work on projects for long periods of time.

Language develops at a very fast pace during this time. Preschoolers begin to use new vocabulary and more complex sentences as they express their ideas more precisely. As their experiences expand, they become increasingly interested in books, print, "writing," and the communication process.

Brain Development During the Early Years

Early childhood educators and neurologists agree that the first eight years in a child's life are a critical time for brain development. Infants are born with a brain that is ready to be woven into a complex system made up of dendrites, neurons, and axons. While some neurons in the brain are wired before birth, many are programmed by early experiences. These early experiences, combined with a child's physical and caring environment, influence brain development. Children who have severely limited opportunities for appropriate experiences during these early years may be delayed in brain development, which may affect future learning. Children who have a rich learning environment, on the other hand, are more likely to achieve their potential.

New research indicates that during a child's early years, there are important "windows of opportunity"—prime times for specific brain development and the making of particular connections. Experts have identified several areas of development that are critical during the early years, including language, logical thinking, music, vision, and emotion. When

Kindergarteners expanding their environment

"It's necessary that we believe that the child is very intelligent, that the child is strong and beautiful...this is the image of the child that we need to hold." (Loris Malaguzzi, 1993)

children have meaningful experiences in these specific areas, there is a positive impact on their current development as well as in the making of important brain connections that last a lifetime.

Auditory Environment

During early childhood, children are sensitive to the sounds and voices in their world. For example, music stimulates the brains of young children. Therefore, it is very important to include music throughout the day in an early childhood environment. By including a variety of music types and musical instruments in the environment, you can expand the sound world of young children as they listen to pitch, rhythm, and pattern. Singing in circle time and during transitions encourages children to discriminate sounds and identify familiar patterns. Making music with simple rhythm instruments lets children connect the object with the sound it produces. Vocal and instrumental recordings and musical instruments provide additional listening experiences that expand the auditory environment for young children.

Preschooler playing an Ashiko African hand drum

Spaces and places that are filled with too much noise or large numbers of children can overload the developing auditory connections in the child's brain. Constant loud sounds can desensitize the child's hearing and interfere with the development of his auditory discrimination. Quiet spaces, separated from loud areas, provide an escape for the child who finds auditory sounds overwhelming. Teachers can use certain materials and techniques in the classroom to soften the sounds or confine loud activities to certain areas of the room. For example, use soft surfaces, such as carpet, fabric, and perforated ceiling tile, to reduce the noise level in a classroom that is built out of concrete blocks and tile flooring. Hard surfaces reflect the sound's intensity while soft materials absorb the sound.

A classroom quilt created by using each child's favorite fabric

Visual Environment

Children develop visual acuity during the first eight years of their lives. As they begin to experience interesting visual images, their perception of objects, movement, and print expands. Experts say that 60% of children's learning occurs through visual and tactile experiences. Children are intrigued and pay attention to visual changes in their environment. A young child's environment should include interesting visual stimulation, such as beautiful paintings, displays, and panels on the wall. As children move about their classroom, they can examine the visually intriguing content of the displays. Organize and position visual displays in interesting ways so that children can appreciate their design.

Colorful and textured displays entice children to examine them. Labeling materials with pictures or words helps the child to "see" the items and understand their organization.

Documentation panel of a walk on campus

Integrated Environment

As young children participate in meaningful activities, they make many connections in their brains. Integrated activities that connect to different types of learning are particulary effective for young children. These experiences stimulate several portions of the child's brain, making connections for meaningful learning. For example, when a child prepares a meal in the Housekeeping Center, he engages in several curriculum areas. He may count the number of eggs needed in the recipe (math), talk to other children about what food to include in the meal (oral language), and observe how the water changes as he washes dishes (science). His play provides the opportunity to develop learning in many areas as he participates in the planning and preparation of an imaginary meal.

An effective early childhood program (programme) includes many opportunities for integrated learning to occur. Learning centers, thematic approaches, and projects are particularly powerful in providing integrated learning and building connections in the brain. Use open-ended materials that allow children to make choices and explore varied ideas.

Emotional Environment

During the child's first years of life, his emotions are strongly influenced by the caregiver's responsiveness. The child's sense of security is strengthened if the caregiver reflects the child's joy, reciprocating his emotions. If the child's feelings are interpreted as annoying by the caregiver, he becomes confused. A caring and responsive caregiver provides a positive climate for the child, which impacts not only his emotional security but also other aspects of his

cognitive development. A child who feels secure and supported will experiment, try new things, and express his ideas freely. A psychologically safe and supportive environment is essential for developing young children as they meet the challenges of each new day.

3-year-old pouring her milk

Independent Learners

An independent learner is one who is able to make personal choices and carry out an appropriate plan of action. Beginning in infancy and toddlerhood, the child has a growing desire to become an independent person, and as he grows and develops, he wants to do things for himself and in his own way. Preschoolers continue in this development process, becoming increasingly competent in making choices, creating a plan, and following through with a project. If children's ideas are valued, they will often work independently on projects for long periods of time. The children are able to revisit and reflect upon their plan, while using their knowledge in meaningful ways to support a long-term learning process.

"A good learning environment empowers children to become confident learners."
(Jim Greenman, 1998)

An effective environment is designed so even the youngest children can be independent. Provide children with many opportunities throughout the day to be successful, as they work to do things for themselves. Providing an orderly display of accessible play materials and creative options helps children understand that they are capable of making decisions. As children grow in their independence, they will select the materials they need.

Exploration of clay with the addition of water

Behaviors (Behaviours) of Children

The environment "tells" children how to act and respond. For example, a large, open space in the middle of the classroom invites children to run across it, while undefined learning center spaces encourage children to wander in and out of areas with little involvement in play. In addition, if only a few materials are available in a play area, children may argue and fight over items. Room arrangement and material availability determine where children focus on their work. It also influences the number of personal interactions children have and the way the group works together. Children learn to respect their environment when given opportunities to interact with beautiful objects and materials. For example, play materials made of hard plastic invite children to be rough with them. On the other hand, if a beautiful flower arrangement is on the table, children are encouraged to look at the display and gently handle the delicate blooms. Children learn to work cooperatively when a space is designed to encourage positive interactions and is effectively arranged to support these efforts.

Children respond differently to the environment. An effectively designed classroom has the potential for positively influencing all areas of children's development: physical, social/emotional, and cognitive. The environment can support the development of behaviors that are valued in our society, such as cooperation and persistence. An aesthetically pleasing space can help children develop an appreciation for the beautiful world. A quality environment can provide a warm setting that "feels" like a good place to be, for many hours and many days.

A beautiful flower, tenderly touched

A bag of treasures brought from home

A Place to Begin: Adding Beauty to the Place

There are many beautiful objects in children's worlds. Set up a low table or countertop to organize and display these materials. Bring in fresh flowers, a collection of nuts, feathers, or interesting fabric pieces. Arrange the articles so children can experience the visual impact of beauty in their world. Children and parents can contribute items that they think are beautiful to expand appreciation of diverse materials. Talk with children about the new display and the beautiful things that are in their space.

Chapter 2

Contemporary Childcare Spaces

An Overview of Current Childcare Spaces

In the past, early childhood classrooms were often an "accidental happening" that was based on the structure of the physical space and available materials. Many classrooms were small rooms, so filled to capacity with supplies, tables, and chairs, that often there was no place for children to focus on their play or work. Seldom was there a place for children to rest their eyes from all the visual stimulation, and even fewer places to provide quiet moments alone. Although these classrooms were functional, they were sometimes chaotic and not very aesthetically appealing.

Another Way to Look at the Early Childhood Classroom

Many educators throughout the world have begun to visit and study the impressive early childhood environments of the Italian Reggio Emilia schools. Educators in the Reggio Emilia schools believe that "the environment is the third teacher." These inspiring educators have shown us what a beautiful environment can be like for young children and have reminded us, in North America, to take a new look at spaces for our young children. By examining their spaces, educators have begun to understand the powerful potential of the environment in an early childhood program and its impact upon all who work there.

Educators in the Reggio Emilia schools have helped us become more aware of the beauty that is possible in early childhood settings. They also have helped us recognize that classroom spaces are used by three different groups of people: children, teachers, and parents. Each group has unique needs that impact the design of the early childhood environment.

The Children in the Environment

Infants, toddlers, and preschoolers use every inch of space in a center (centre). In many settings, children between the ages of six to twelve in after-school programs also use the center. How can you design a space that meets the needs of this wide age range of children?

Children of every age learn in unique ways and have needs that are specific to their stage of development. Infants and toddlers are in the sensory motor stage of development. They require places to fulfill their basic needs of eating, changing, and sleeping. They also need space to explore physically and visually, so their environment must be both safe and stimulating. The areas must provide them with opportunities to examine and manipulate real things, as well as the space to practice their emerging motor skills, such as crawling, walking, pushing, and pulling. They need soft materials for stroking, hard surfaces for pulling themselves up, and pictures and materials at their eye level.

Friendships develop in a nurturing environment.

You should design the classroom environment of preschool children to meet their unique needs, and clearly demonstrate that this is a place where young children live and work. Display their pictures and work to communicate their ownership to all who visit the classroom. The preschooler's space should support their active and independent learning. To encourage a sense of community, include places for group meetings, planning, and reflecting, and provide many opportunities for large and small groups to work together. Design learning centers to nurture language, social development, and cognitive abilities. These centers, and other small group activities, encourage language exploration and the sharing of ideas that lead to cooperative play. Young children are very curious and need to manipulate the real items in their world. Therefore, make natural materials easily accessible so children can examine them visually and physically.

Each child should recognize that this place is specifically "for me," that it is designed for him and supports his way of learning. By displaying children's pictures and work throughout the space, you convey respect to the experiences that happen in this space and the individuals who live in this space.

Teachers and Staff in the Environment

Most early childhood centers focus primarily on the needs of children in the program. Very little concern is directed to you—the teachers and staff who work in this environment. You spend a major portion of your time in this space, too. Throughout the day, you try to squeeze into tiny chairs, eat from low tables, and find someplace to converse with an adult.

Display with pictures of toddlers in the classroom

As teachers and staff, you want to be in a pleasant working environment that addresses your special adult needs. You need a place to keep personal belongings, as well as a comfortable place to take a break and revitalize your energy. In addition, designating a meeting space for all teachers to work together and share information about children encourages collaboration.

Each classroom should be unique, shaped by the people who live in it. Include items that you enjoy in your classroom, such as personal materials, tapes/discs, and books. Display pictures of family or vacations, or other special objects in the center or classroom for everybody's enjoyment. In the welcoming area of the center or classroom, display information and pictures of all the staff and teachers. This panel demonstrates your importance and influence on the development of a quality program.

When teachers and staff are valued, it demonstrates respect for their special contribution to the program. It also shows that you and children are both important partners in this shared place.

The teachers and staff in the early childhood program

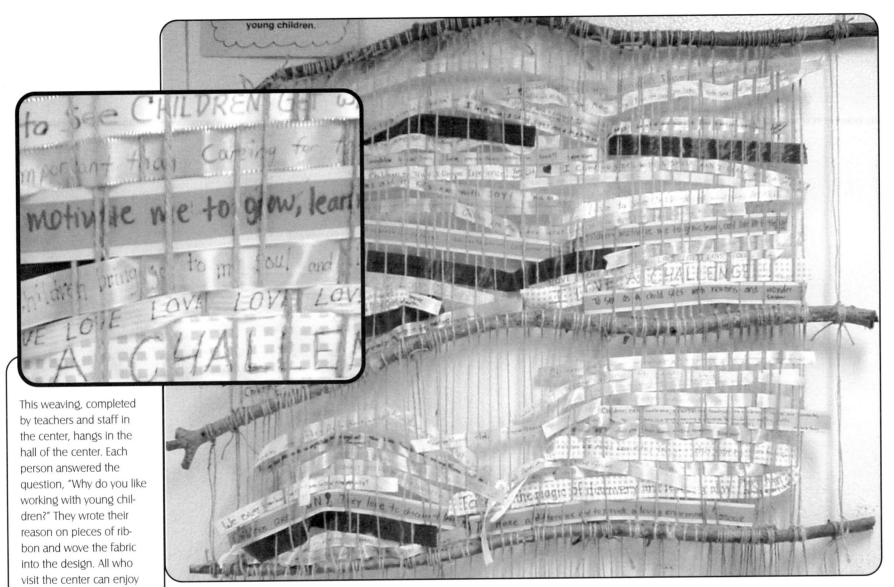

This weaving, completed by teachers and staff in the center, hangs in the hall of the center. Each person answered the question, "Why do you like working with young children?" They wrote their reason on pieces of ribbon and wove the fabric into the design. All who visit the center can enjoy this beautiful weaving.

"The environment is not just beautiful but highly personalized."
(Lella Gandini, 1984)

Parents

Parents are an important part of the early childhood environment, too. They have special needs that should impact the design of space. For example, when parents bring their children in the morning or pick them up in the afternoon, acknowledge them and make them feel welcome. Is there a place for them to easily store their children's clothing or other belongings? Is there a place for them to relax if they arrive early? Where do they wait while their child is deeply involved in an activity? Efforts to meet these needs help parents feel that they are important members of the school community.

A father and daughter entering the classroom

Parents want to know what their children are doing in the classroom. Often, they want to learn patterns of "normal" child development. To support parents' desire to be part of their children's education, set up a centrally located "library" area of parent materials, books, and videos and allow them to borrow items. This accessible arrangement allows parents to select what interests them and read about personally relevant issues.

Parents want to know the people who are working in the center and influencing their children's lives. Display information about teachers and staff, including their training and interests, so parents can learn about each person's special abilities.

Displays of children's work, with documentation of their language and interactions, help parents understand the learning that is occurring in the program.

Newsletters, parent meetings, conferences, and social happenings within the center assist parents and teachers in making important connections. As each learns about the other, mutual respect and support grows. Parents have many special abilities and talents to share, so invite them to visit, participate, and work with children on projects. This utilizes parents' strengths and helps them become active participants in the early childhood program. Developing a team that includes parents and teachers will strengthen the program and provide many new possibilities for collaboration, which creates a strong environment for young children.

Children, Parents, and Teachers

There is a growing understanding that the "best" early childhood environments consider the needs of the three important groups using the space—children, teachers, and parents. A child-centered place recognizes the unique capabilities of each child. It also supports a community of learners that values the special abilities of children, teachers, and parents.

The shared space for children, teachers, and parents should be warm, home-like, and inviting, with beautiful and natural materials. When you design the environment around the needs of children, teachers, and parents, you clearly demonstrate a climate of respect and that this is a place that matters.

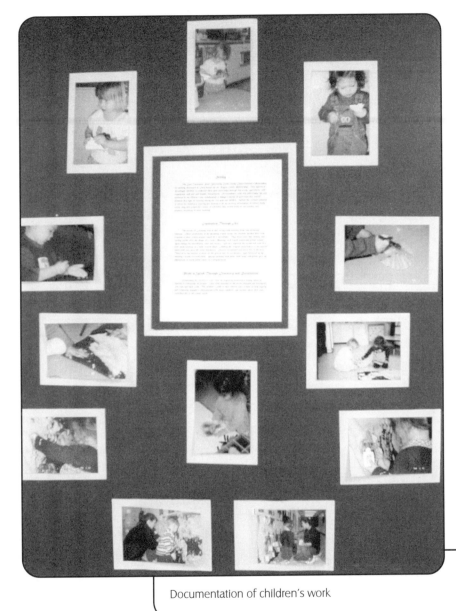

Documentation of children's work

Sign-in and informational area for parents and children

A Place to Begin: Teachers and Staff Display

Collect photographs of all of the teachers and staff that the children see each day. Make frames out of cardboard or poster board for each person's picture. Decorate each frame in unique ways using fabric, foil, contact paper, heavy yarn, dried flowers, or crushed tissue paper. Write a short paragraph about each person under his or her beautiful frame. Arrange the framed pictures in an attractive, organized pattern and place the display close to the entrance of the center or classroom.

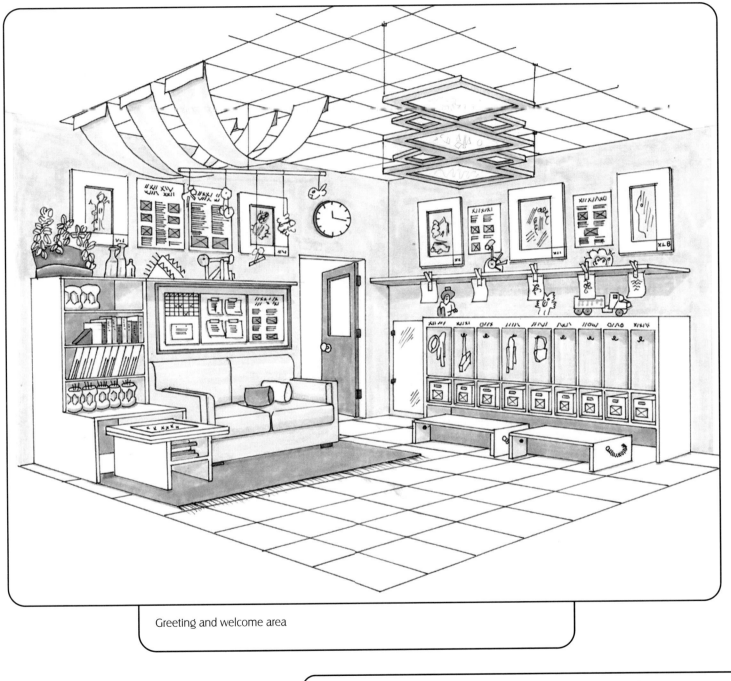

Greeting and welcome area

The Teacher's New Role: Designer

chapter 3

An attractive display that includes the children's projects on castles

Early childhood educators are masters of many skills. We wear a number of hats—all at the same time. Some of the hats are budget manager, health inspector, toy mender, cook, and maintenance specialist. Have you ever thought of yourself as an interior designer or decorator? For example, do you move furniture often, putting little thought into the aesthetic qualities of space? When was the last time you asked yourself, "Do the colors (colours) harmonize?" or "Do the patterned fabrics go together?" Have you thought about the lighting in the space? These are the things an interior designer would think about. Get ready to try on a new hat, interior designer!

An Introduction to Design Principles

Designing involves more than rearranging furnishings in the space to generate new arrangements. For example, you may move furniture around just for the sake of a new look. Or, someone may move the furniture to clean the floor. For some reason, furniture and equipment are rarely returned to their earlier sites.

Think of designing as rearranging and editing. After the initial reorganization, designing should become less rearranging and more editing. Some might even call this a process of "tweaking" the space—making slight modifications to improve the setting rather than making dramatic changes. Think of this task as decorating.

Ground Rules for Well-Designed Spaces for Children

To make a well-designed space for children, consider the following:

1. Designated Space—Each group of children should have a designated space that offers them the feeling of being in their "home base." This space should be a familiar and friendly force in their lives, and it should also support their interests and learning.
2. Variety of Functions—Classroom spaces serve a number of functions, including:
   Playroom
   Sleep room
   Lunchroom
   Storage
   Meeting room
   Music room
   Gymnasium
   Art room
   Block center (centre)
   Drama area
   Library
   Science Center
   Woodworking/Carpentry

Science exploration

3. Space for all Seasons of the Year—Places in the classroom to enjoy natural materials during each of the seasons, including a place to use when the weather is inclement.

4. Washroom—These facilities should be near the classroom to permit greater independence for the children. Sinks should be child-height or easily accessible.

5. Washable Flooring—Appropriate flooring that you can easily wash is essential for overall good sanitation and health.

6. Warm Floors—Uncarpeted floor areas should be warmed by radiant heating. Use carpets or area rugs where appropriate.

7. Aesthetically Pleasing—Make sure the patterns, textures, colors, and design elements in the classroom are visually pleasing.

8. Visual Complexity—Provide a variety of colors, textures, different levels, and sensory variations in the classroom.

9. Windows at the Child's Level—Clean all the windowpanes and make sure all the windows at the child's level are protected.

10. Open and Inviting Entrance Area—An open and inviting entrance area offers an invitation to all children, parents, and visitors.

11. Flexible Use of Furnishings—Select furnishings that you can easily move and rearrange.

12. Acoustical Materials—Use a variety of soft materials, such as curtains, rugs, tiles, and carpet.

13. Direct and Indirect Lighting—Balance direct and indirect lighting with small lamps and light strips.

14. Balance of Child-Scaled and Adult-Sized Furnishing—Include both sizes of furnishings in the classroom.

15. Abundance of Child-Accessible Spaces—Provide many opportunities for children to select spaces for play activities.

16. Uncovered Floor Space—Keep one third of the floor space uncarpeted to encourage floor play, transitions, and messy activities.

17. Clear Pathways—Provide easy transition pathways between play areas and work areas.

18. Well-Defined Activity Areas—Use boundaries and dividers to establish areas.

19. Sufficient Materials Stored Near Activity Area—Provide open storage units that are visible and accessible.

20. Safe Areas and Materials—Make sure that all areas and materials are safe. Constantly monitor the environment and remove broken toys.

How to Begin Classroom Transformations

If you determine that your classroom environment needs transformation and attention, the following steps will be helpful to you.

Goals

To guide your thinking and activities, it is valuable to set goals for any project. Setting goals is an important step in the change process and provides you with the focus of the plan. Keep in mind that you can revise your goals when needed.

Collect Information

To make your goals meaningful, you must have a solid understanding of why they are necessary. Think about what is happening in your classroom. For several days, record what happens and how the space influences what takes place. For instance, you may notice that as children make their way from one area to another, several children bump into an activity table. You may have been unaware this was happening, so note the event in your personal journal. Collecting information may seem like a chore, but you will gain a new understanding of how the classroom functions.

Furniture Notes

A good first step is to review the state of the room's furnishings. Inspect and record the condition of all the classroom furniture. Make a note of what needs to be painted or replaced. One teacher had never looked carefully at the chairs in her room. When she did, she noted that they needed to be scrubbed. Her first mini-goal was to wash the chairs, which she easily achieved without spending any money.

Sensory Notes

List the things in your classroom that stimulate the senses of sight, touch, hearing, taste, and smell. A good example would be the aroma of your classroom when you first open the door in the morning. Record this sensation and research the topic of scents. For example, it is known that certain odors affect behaviors (behaviours), emotions, and mood. Therefore, environmental fragrance can be an important topic when examining your classroom. Another important sense is touch. What different textures are within your classroom? For example, young children may calm down by stroking soft materials. Or, a rough carpet may discourage children from working on the floor. Varying the surfaces can provide a new dimension to the classroom.

Discover Personal Preference

The best way to get in touch with what appeals to you is to clip magazine pictures. Collect decorating magazines, women's journals, or architectural magazines and look through them to find things that you like and find appealing. You may find a colorful room or an arrangement of pictures that you like. Place the pictures in a box or file, and attach a sticky note or mark the interesting feature with a highlighter pen. Don't give the process much thought—just rip, mark, and drop into the box. When you mark the clippings, you begin to reveal themes of personal interest.

A Design Reference Collection

Your personal preference clippings can form the foundation of your design reference collection. It is helpful to look at what others have done in different settings, so organize and revisit these files when you need new inspiration. Think of the design reference collection as your professional picture file. Clip additional pictures of large areas of rooms from magazines. (These images are often full- or half-page illustrations.) Carefully examine them to gather creative ideas to use in your classroom. Focus on the use of color, design, texture, and display.

When you have a substantial number of images in your collection, cut and mount them on paper or cardboard. Leave the images whole or use strips, swatches, or shapes. Review the images to develop new inspirations and ideas. Identify new details and continue to work with the arrangement. Begin to think about how you can transfer these beautiful environments to your classroom setting.

An Accessory Idea File

In addition to a design reference collection, you should also make an accessory idea file. This is a file of the accessories, or smaller items, that offer a sense of individuality and uniqueness to children's spaces. Cut out pictures from larger photos and mount the images on large file cards. You may gather ideas ranging from making fabric-covered picture frames to handcrafted storage containers. Other examples are how to create a unique bulletin board or how to sew soft pillows. Some of the ideas may require the skills of a seamstress, carpenter, or craftsperson.

This collection of accessory ideas will help you focus on creative possibilities and the inclusion of things of beauty. Sources for these possibilities include catalogs (catalogues), woodworking magazines, design magazines, women's magazines, and pattern books.

Collect images of accessories that can be added to a childcare environment. These pictures might include bookends, wall hangings, bench covers, beanbag chairs, and storage bags. Look for items that are visually interesting and innovative. You may need to modify some items for use in the classroom, and some items will function as a catalyst for generating other ideas.

Topics for the Design Reference Collection and the Accessory Idea File

Listed below are ideas for the design reference collection and the accessory file.

- Visual images that have interesting colors and/or shapes
- Environments that exhibit a coordinated color palette

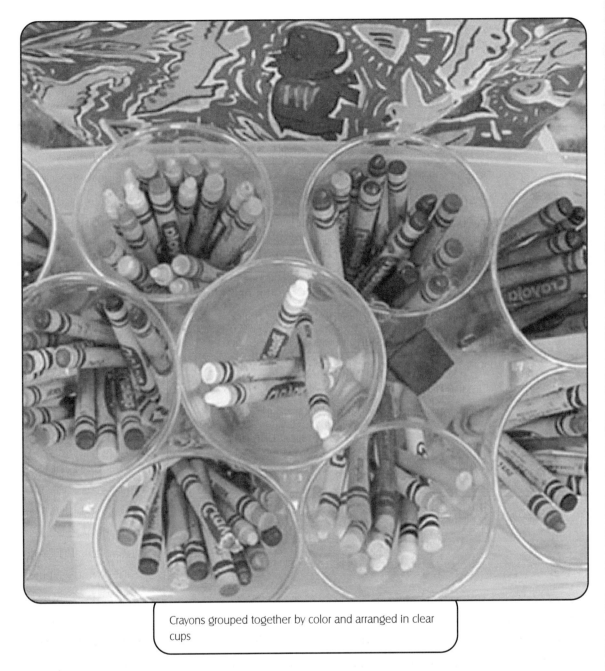

Crayons grouped together by color and arranged in clear cups

- Diagrams for making accessories
- Renovations or alterations made to spaces
- Ideas for changing furniture
- Creative play materials with directions
- Space analysis projects
- Interesting environmental photos
- Lighting
- Windows
- Doorways
- Floors and their coverings
- Rich, stimulating environments—texture, color, and so on
- New construction vs. renovation
- How to arrange a space
- Spaces for equipment and materials
- Designs for safety
- Improving spaces

A Place to Begin: Take a Designer's Look

Take a few moments to look at your classroom with new eyes. In the past, your view of the classroom environment probably has been focused on the functions of the space. Begin to look closer at the factors that influence the design and aesthetic appearance of your space.

Do you want to create a beautiful environment for you and your children? This simple survey will help you begin to "see" your classroom in new ways.

1. When you enter the classroom, do you see an attractive space?
2. Do children have a place that feels like home?
3. Is there a neutral background, with color providing accents?
4. Are children's materials grouped together in attractive ways?
5. How many different textures are in the space?
6. Do you have rugs and pillows to soften the space?
7. Did you display children's work in an attractive, organized way?
8. Have you discovered the way light enters your room during the day?
9. Do you have living plants in the classroom?
10. Are interesting items hanging from the ceiling?
11. Can you identify all who live and work in this space?
12. Is there something beautiful in your classroom?

The Block/Construction area

chapter 4

Principles of Meaningful Environments

Meaningful Childcare Environments

A meaningful environment has spaces with assigned purposes. In childcare, space plays many different roles—it is a place to play, eat, and sleep. It is also a place for children to belong and learn.

When designing and arranging an early childhood environment, you place many expectations on the space. First, you want the environment to meet the developmental needs and requirements of the children. You also want everyone who enters the space to gain meaning from every arrangement, ranging from the type of furniture in the room to live plants. The classroom setting is also intended to be a place where ideas are shared, as well as a place where children can see and use a variety of play materials. This environment is where exploration and new discoveries happen each day.

Does It Matter?

The interpretations and expectations of space often vary from teacher to teacher and region to region. Yet teachers, directors, and others are beginning to put more thought and consideration into the spaces where children spend the greater part of their day. Budget dollars are being allotted to furnishing and maintaining these spaces. In addition, a few industries have become interested in childcare environments, because they realize that businesses continue to prosper, in part, because childcare programs exist. Educational supply houses also have begun to focus on the needs of early childhood programs.

Some childcare settings are very small while others are large. Some centers (centres) are well furnished and equipped, while others function with minimal materials. Regardless of their size or furnishings, childcare settings must be meaningful spaces for children.

Today's parents are becoming more informed childcare consumers. Many are developing a discerning eye as they search for and select care for their children. As the number of parent-consumers increases, they will impact the way childcare centers function.

Society in general is also beginning to view children's spaces as important places. More and more educators are examining how to develop childcare spaces and the impression it conveys to everyone who uses it. These spaces must be comfortable and appropriate places for children, teachers, and parents.

Materials for Children

Materials in the childcare setting should be varied. Include open-ended materials that children can use in many different ways and simple items for them to combine to allow for more complex play. Extend the items beyond traditional toys and include materials that fall into the category of delicate, beautiful, and special. Make sure the materials offer interesting color (colour), textures, and varied designs. These features will enhance the usual collection of childcare furniture, equipment, and supplies.

A beautiful collection of smooth stones

How to Recognize a Meaningful Environment

A childcare space transmits many messages. The environment reveals your decisions about its appearance and functions. For example, the color of the room clearly sends a message of "feeling," such as cool, cheery, or quiet. Wherever children, teachers, and parents gather to share time and experiences, they use the space in a meaningful way. Enhance these interactions through attention to detail and a professional sense of responsibility for the development of the environment.

A Child's Sense of Space

Children like to explore the spaces and materials that they encounter. They derive great pleasure from making discoveries and learning about the unique characteristics of the area. When designing an environment that supports play, provide child-level, reachable storage and sufficient spaces for children to move and work—storage and play areas that are organized and consistent within the space. Spaces and activity centers that support children's independence and decision-making allow them to make the environment their own.

Generating a Feeling of Home

Recent research in child development and childcare settings has raised concerns about the impact of the early childhood environment on children. Some early childhood programs recognize the value of using elements and furnishings often found in homes. Rugs, plants, and lamps are just a few of the items that generate a desirable softening of the spaces. These new additions help the environment become less institutional and more inviting. Moving from the institutional model to a more home-like environment can have a positive impact on children, teachers, and parents.

A soft chair provides a special place for enjoying books

A Plan of Action

Childcare settings are places where large numbers of individuals arrive each day to participate in a variety of activities, such as teachers supporting children's learning and parents' developing parenting skills, children enjoying the daily activities and play spaces, and teachers and parents sharing experiences and observations.

For environments to be growing and learning places of the highest quality, all who use it should be responsible for and interested in the development of the center. Some teachers have the training and understanding of what quality environments for young children can be like. These teachers could generate preliminary plan and ideas. Others, however, may need help in developing the environment and understanding the essential elements.

Getting the Help of Parents

One way to gain assistance for environmental improvements is to include parents in the plan. By including parents and asking them to donate materials and skills, you will achieve an individualized and unique setting. In one center, teachers listed what they needed, such as baskets, fabric, and plants. They posted the list on the classroom door and sent a copy home with each child. Parents generously brought in their donations and placed them in a box. The children were delighted to sort through the materials, and they often noted, "This is from my home!" The children and teachers placed the donations throughout the classroom, which helped transform the space. Parents were pleased and were soon making suggestions and inquiries, and identifying other items that might be useful in the classroom. Before

long, the teachers and parents were actively collaborating and assessing the results of their joint efforts. Successful experiences like this can lead to other partnerships with parents and teachers.

A mother watches as her child irons fabric for the wall hanging.

Differences in Play

Introducing unique materials that are not usually found in childcare settings can have a dramatic impact. Teachers have noted that children handle real and natural materials differently than plastic materials and have been very surprised by these differences.

Why do natural items seem to encourage a different kind of play? Is it novelty? Why do children seem to know that a different method of play or interaction is required? How is it that this newly discovered play behavior (behaviour) lasts for a longer period of time? Perhaps, this comes about through their careful observation of what happens around them.

Making Spaces Beautiful

Natural and real items soften a harsh classroom. Adults, both parents and teachers, can enhance classroom spaces by adding items with individualized personal appeal. For example, one teacher brought in her growing collection of butterfly magnets. Another parent offered to re-pot the classroom plants into clay pots that she had hand-painted with designs that appealed to the children. One child brought in her collection of smooth stones.

Appealing to the Human Senses

Another way to bring newness to a classroom is to put items in the setting that appeal to the senses (touch, smell, sound, and sight)—things that can be experienced in new ways. The opportunity to touch different materials and explore various textures is a positive way for children to learn more about their environment.

When smells are part of the physical space, the child's range of understanding and appreciation is enriched. For example, a bouquet of fresh spring flowers immediately captures the interest of young children as they enjoy the beautiful scent.

Sound also enriches the classroom environment. Soft tones are better than loud noises. Play CDs and tapes of nature sounds or beautiful music to change the environment in special ways. Wind chimes and musical instruments allow children to experience making sounds and producing rhythm patterns.

Color

Visual experiences involve color and light. Because color has emotional appeal, selecting colors for childcare spaces is very subjective. Some general suggestions about how to use color: Although deep color tones are often preferred, it is much better to select a more neutral tone for large areas and walls of the classroom. Neutral colors create the impression that spaces are larger. Use distinct colors to provide accents within the larger space. By using this method, you can display your individual color preferences without having to reapply wall color, an expensive and time-consuming task. Involve children in the selection of colors as well. An excellent way to offer children opportunities to select and learn about color is to hang colored panels from the ceiling or attach them to the walls. Change them as desired, and with ease. They can be painted or fabric-covered pieces of foam board, plywood, or ceiling tile. Other ways to include color variations in

Light and color add interest to the classroom environment.

the classroom are to have pillow covers available for floor and furniture use or area rugs with color and textures.

Use paper color wheels to learn about the intricacies of primary, secondary, and intermediate colors. Color wheels are a valuable tool for artists, designers, interior decorators, or anyone involved in color selection and application. You can learn to learn to distinguish tint colors (when white is added to a color) from shades (when black is added to a color).

If you wish to explore your own color preferences, there are a number of published works on this topic. Although personal preferences will definitely influence your views about using color in the classroom, begin to see room color as a background for display, and use color to draw attention to specific features or items.

Light

The need for light within a space is determined by the amount of light available from outside sources. A secondary consideration is the physical location and layout of artificial light. In settings for children, it is highly desirable to have both light and dark areas within the space. The book area, for example, requires brighter light than other areas, such as the block area or dramatic play center, where lighting can be less intense. The amount of lighting needed also depends on the color of the floor or other large surfaces in the room. For example, dark-colored flooring absorbs light, so you need neutral-colored walls, ceilings, and windows to achieve balance. Another consideration in determining lighting needs is the size and shape of the room. A simple solution to providing lighting variations within a classroom is to replace a regular light switch (toggle) with a dimmer switch. Another alternative is to use incandescent area lamps that simulate a soft home-like environment.

When a room's lighting fixture is placed in the center of the space, you can be certain that the corners of the room are inadequately lit. At the opposite extreme is the brightness produced by the massive use of artificial fluorescent ceiling units. These banks of lights can be visually uncomfortable and over-stimulating to both children and adults. Experts in lighting recommend full-spectrum lighting in classroom environments. Exchange cool white tubes, which are usually found in the classroom, for warm white or full spectrum tubes. Use low light for casual reading or

Clamp lights add interest to a dark corner.

work, medium light for prolonged concentration, and bright light for close work with small details.

The intensity of light on a work surface depends on the brightness of the lamp and its distance from the task. The brightness of light increases dramatically as it is brought closer to the task. Some areas of the classroom reflect more light than other parts of the room. Black and white are considered reflective extremes—white reflects a lot of light while black does not.

Natural light is another lighting design issue in the classroom setting. It continually changes throughout the day. You can control the amount of natural light with a variety of window coverings that prevent glare, such as shades, blinds, or curtains. Light filtering into a room offers an aesthetic source of illumination, as well as variety and change. Depending on the direction of the light source or the nature of the glass, skylights and windows can be either a source of pleasure or irritation.

Mirrors offer a feeling of openness and are invaluable for making spaces appear larger. They have a reflective quality that brings light into dark spaces to increase lighting intensity.

They also allow children to see themselves and their work from different perspectives.

Open and Transparent

When designing an environment for young children, it is important to consider a new characteristic—transparency. Transparency refers to how light enters a space and allows children to see spaces more clearly. In the past, the focus was on accessibility—making sure materials were close to where children used them and placed at a level that children could reach. Now, in addition, it is recognized that it is important to make materials more visible and store them in clear containers that allow children to understand their organization.

Transparent storage containers give children the opportunity to see all the available choices and the interesting designs created by the open display. In the art/studio area, for example, display trim materials in clear jars. The children can see red pompoms, silver strips of paper, buttons, and colored pieces of fabric, each in their own separate clear container. An attractive, open display like this helps children to make choices and enjoy the beauty and variety of the materials.

Impact of Arrangement

Grouping and arranging furnishings within an environment helps children make associations with spaces. These activity areas are clearly defined by the way you position shelving, furniture, and dividers, which helps children understand where the play occurs. Group materials and furnishings related to particular activities to form centers, zones, or play areas.

Make sure that pathways through the room are reasonably direct and avoid pathways that extend the full length of the room. Clear pathways keep traffic away from activity areas and do not disrupt children's involvement in their work.

Environmental Decoration

The decoration of a space can range from adding accessory items to suspending fabric from the ceiling to mounting pictures on the wall. For example, wallpaper borders—near the ceiling, midway on a wall, or at the baseboard level—can add interest to the space. However, because it has limited durability and requires frequent renewal (at considerable expense), only use it in select locations. Be sure to include items that reflect the culture of the children and their families. Unique and special accessories can create a bond between the classroom space and the community. Personalize the environment by including fabrics, ornamentation, pictures, and food that reflect the children, teachers, and parents of the class.

A Place to Pause

Children's spaces are busy places. However, children need places to pause or remove themselves from the busy activity of the moment. Good mental health requires one to spend time away from others now and then. To create some places to pause, display interesting items on the windowsills, tables, or shelves for children to examine. Choose items that are not overly fragile but require careful handling. A table or cabinet (cupboard) dedicated to nature and science works well. You might include a secluded and quiet spot for the child to watch fish swim in an aquarium. Or, create a growing centercontaining blooming plants as another place to pause and reflect.

The Music area

A Place to Rest

Young children are busy almost every minute of their day. Provide a number of resting spots within the classroom that children can select. Pillows and a mattress in a quiet corner, along with a collection of interesting books, is one way to offer rest opportunities. Another simple option is to provide a fabric curtain over a cabinet or closet. Inside this space, include a thick floorpad and pillows to encourage slowing down and resting. These types of places will help children develop responsibility for their need to rest.

A Place for Communicating

A loft provides a special space for sharing books and talking. Loft areas or raised platforms provide unique opportunities for verbal exchanges between children. These are special places where children can get together and talk within a busy classroom setting. The physical detachment of the loft offers a sense of separation while allowing them visual contact with the rest of the setting. The size of the space limits the number of children that can be in the area, providing more opportunity for private interactions.

A Place for Work and Play

Generally, classrooms are divided into meaningful places for both work and play. Tables, platforms, and the floor provide the best places for children to engage in play or special activities. If you have space available, use drapery or taller furniture to separate it from the rest of the room to provide quiet work areas for art activities, socio-dramatic play, or enjoying a book.

"Interest areas are well defined and arranged to minimize conflict and maximize interaction with materials and peers." (Verna Hildebrand, 1984)

Teacher and children reading in a loft area.

Personal Things and Personal Places

Environments for young children must be responsive to their needs and to the items that are personally meaningful to them. If childcare settings are to have a positive impact on the development of children, then the space must address the personal and individualized needs of each child. There must be places in the setting for children to keep items with personal value. The item might be a tiny toy from a box of breakfast cereal, a stuffed animal, or a favorite (favourite) storybook. These items may be of great value to the child. Perhaps the rule that stipulates, "these things must not come to school" should be reconsidered.

To possess things is a vital and significant element of being human. Adults own and value things—children do too. They collect things and want to include them in their space. How can teachers provide places for children's creative efforts, as well as for items of intrinsic and personal value? Personal places may be as simple as providing a plastic bin in the bottom of a cubby. This simple addition provides children with a place to visit and cherish these special items during the day.

Creating special storage for personal items

A Case Study: The Reggio Emilia Approach

In recent years, educators from around the world have become aware of the quality programs found in Reggio Emilia. This northern Italian community of 300,000 has created a municipally operated childcare system that is the envy of all who have come to visit. Over the last 15 years, conferences, workshops, and exhibits held in the United States and Canada have enabled North Americans to begin to appreciate the Reggio approach to early childhood education. Numerous childcare sites across the continent have implemented their interpretation of the Reggio approach in their own environments. Some schools or childcare programs (programmes) have even sent teachers to visit the Reggio Emilia schools.

What Makes the Reggio Emilia Approach Unique?

The 33 municipal schools of Reggio Emilia offer full-day care for children from infancy through preschool. These schools have teachers who have maintained their positions for long periods of time—even several decades. Children and teachers progress together from one classroom to another throughout the child's three-year stay in the infant/toddler school. At the end of this program, children move to a new school for the next three years. Once again, as children mature, their teacher moves with them to new classrooms.

As teachers progress with the children from one level to another, they gain a detailed understanding of each child. This helps to explain how teachers are able to design such a dynamic and meaningful curriculum. Teachers record their many interactions and conversations with the children. Then, they review these observations and create documentation panels with photographs and written commentary. When parents and visitors look at these panels, they gain a unique and detailed insight into the workings of the program.

Teachers are attentive to children's many interests. They offer support and encourage children's long and detailed explorations of diverse topics. They encourage children to work cooperatively in classroom spaces that offer a wide range of materials. Some of these materials are purchased, but many are recycled items, such as rope, yard, fabric, and boxes. Teachers present and use these recycled items in unique ways. In addition, parents and/or teachers have crafted a significant number of the play items.

Parents and teachers cultivate an environment that offers many different play opportunities in an architecturally interesting space. A great deal of care and attention is given to these childcare spaces. For example, children make use of materials that can be found in the day-to-day world of family life, such as pots, pans, and dishes.

Reggio Emilia teachers spend considerable time attending to how to display and organize materials. In particular, they are very sensitive to how color and texture relate to each other. It shows in their environments. All who visit the Reggio sites are amazed at their beauty. These teachers have taken environments and programs for young children to a new level of professionalism.

A Place to Begin: The Art Studio

Take a look at your art center. What materials are typically in this area? There are paints, crayons, glue, scissors, and markers as well as a variety of paper, including manila paper, construction paper, newsprint, and computer paper. What unique materials and tools can you add to this area to encourage creative work?

Unique Material Suggestions

buttons	small boxes
colored cotton balls	small pieces of foam
containers	small pinecones
corks	spools
dried flowers	stones
feathers	strips of colored electrical
film canisters	tape
foil	wood scraps
juice lids	wrapping paper
keys	yarn
old jewelry	
pieces of mesh wire	
pipe cleaners	
ribbon	
scraps of fabric	
seashells	
shiny decorations	

Unique Tool Suggestions

charcoal
cleaning tools
colored pencils
colored tape
combs
eyedroppers
kitchen utensils
large and small brushes
paint rollers
paint scraper
pinking shears
rulers
small spray bottles
stamps
staplers
texture tools
watercolors
weaving frame

Storage Possibilities:
Place selected items in clear containers that allow children to see their possibilities. Then, arrange them in interesting and organized patterns. Prepare a storage area in the studio to provides a place for children to display their work in progress. This also allows them to revisit and refine their work over an extended period of time.

The Art area

chapter 5

Aspects of Quality Environments for Children

Places and Spaces: The Materials Needed to Create Them

Space is a critical component in the creation of a quality environment for young children. The minimum amount of space allocated to an indoor area is usually an approved number of square feet assigned by the regional or state agency responsible for licensing the childcare center (centre). However, the types and amount of materials designated for activity areas, such as art or socio-dramatic, do not fall under such strict guidelines. Selection of these materials is the responsibility of the program director and staff, who often make their selections using catalogs (catalogues) from companies that focus on early childhood education. Of course, the range and type of materials available from these sources is diverse and varies in quality.

For many programs with limited funds, it is often necessary to construct or collect furniture and materials. The selection of age-appropriate materials, purchased or constructed, often depends upon the knowledge and experience of teachers and staff. Their appreciation for various types of toys and materials is based upon their understanding of child development. When this knowledge is combined with careful selection and appropriate funding, the center can be equipped with an excellent array of materials.

When a program (programme) has been operating for some time, it is possible that some items may have been placed in storage and forgotten. A careful check of all storage areas is a good place to begin before developing your latest request for materials. An inventory journal is an excellent way to keep records of the school's equipment and materials. (See Appendix A for a sample Inventory Form.)

A childcare program requires:
- Furniture
- Environmental accessories
- Tools
- Equipment
- Materials (consumables)
- Equipment and supplies for children with special needs

Checklists are another way to monitor the availability of equipment. Each classroom and adjoining area should have an associated checklist (see Appendix B for a sample Equipment Checklist) form including two major categories—basic and optional. Each major indoor activity areas and their materials should have a separate checklist. The key areas are:
- The Art Center
- Dramatic Play (Socio-Dramatic Center)
- Music/Movement
- Sand Play
- Science Center
- Pet Area
- Water Play
- Carpentry Center
- Library Area
- Blocks
- Communication Center

The Communication area

Quality vs. Quantity of Space

Bigger is sometimes equated with better. But in the field of childcare, this is not necessarily correct. Carefully designed small spaces can be more efficient than a large space that lacks sufficient materials. However, a disorganized small area is not a quality environment for young children either. When all elements of the space function together in a harmonious manner, then, and only then, do you have something that approximates quality.

The Configuration and Evaluation of Space

There are many ways to evaluate a space, including how well children can be supervised, how accessible the material in the centers are, and how well the indoor space is set up as a floor plan. For example, when a play area permits easy supervision, from the dimension of space supervision, it is viewed as a quality space. Quality spaces are also well maintained with plentiful play materials. However, if the play items are stored in storage areas, cabinets (cupboards), and closets, the space would be considered poor because the materials are not easily accessible and must be retrieved by adults from a variety of storage places.

When a number of program elements are consistently rated high, it is possible for the entire setting to receive a high rating. It is important for teachers to understand how the program achieves this evaluation. Another important consideration for teachers and staff is how to maintain this quality over time.

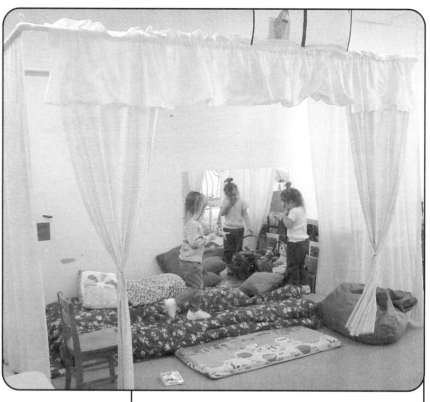

Suspended fabric can create a very unique area for play.

Materials and Furnishings

Type and Quality

An important factor related to the quality of a program for young children is the type and appropriateness of materials and furnishings. Materials are expendable—they are used up in the natural flow of caring for and educating young children. For example, construction paper, white glue, and clay are consumable materials. In addition, some materials become worn out or broken.

Furnishings and equipment, however, are long-term investments. These items should be more durable and often are more costly. Regardless of their cost, the intent always should be to obtain the best possible value for durability and long-term use.

Criteria for Choosing Items for Children's Use
1. Attractive and pleasing to the eye and touch
2. Retains the interest of children
3. Multiple uses (open-ended)
4. Sturdy/Durable
5. Washable
6. Good design
7. Quality workmanship
8. Safe for use by children
9. Cost effective

Safety

Whether you are purchasing or constructing items, your goal is for all items to be safe for the group they serve: young children, infants, or toddlers. When possible, scale large items to children's size. For example, shorten the legs of an attractive wooden table so the top is an appropriate height for preschoolers. When shortening is not possible, employ other strategies. For example, when an adult-sized sink is the only one available, one strategy is to construct a well-secured step-up platform at the sink. Other items that children use must be unbreakable, non-brittle, and stable.

Provide only non-toxic paint for young children to use, and be sure the surfaces of equipment in the classroom are painted with non-toxic paint. This is an important consideration when teachers or parent groups are constructing equipment and will be painting or finishing the items.

Cleanliness

Teachers in quality environments take great care to insure that all items handled by young children can be washed or laundered. This is the first level of the process of sanitizing items to eliminate germs. There are many products available for the sanitizing processes that are safe for use in a childcare environment.

Cleanliness involves more than sanitizing; it also includes how items appear. Are they clean or stained? How well is the floor maintained? Most programs do not have a daytime custodian, so the staff does the day-to-day cleaning. In a busy and demanding environment, attention to careful cleaning of windows or washing walls may be neglected. If so, it is highly likely that the childcare setting does not present a well-kept image. This can impact health issues and the public perception of the center.

It is important, however, to remember that many of the wonderful experiences that children need are messy. These opportunities are essential components of the curriculum and should be valued. Sand and water areas are good examples of messy areas that provide meaningful learning. Here, children learn the properties of sand by pouring, sifting, and tunneling. Of course, a consequence of this activity is sand and/or water on the floor around the area. Plan ways to contain the sand by placing plastic on the floor so the clean up is less demanding. Children can use a broom and dustpan or a rechargeable, battery-operated hand vacuum. Children who live in a clean and well-organized environment will actively participate in the care of their space.

Maintenance

Maintenance of an environment is an important consideration in establishing a well-cared-for appearance. For example, clean, non-chipped walls demonstrate that an environment is carefully maintained. A well maintained setting conveys a subtle message to children: This is an important place, and we value how it looks. It also has a positive effect on the morale of the teachers and staff who live in this place.

Quality Standards

Teachers must maintain the standards implemented by state or regional licensing agents. Some of these standards are high and impact quality, while others offer only minimal requirements in the childcare setting. Professional organizations often support higher standards that have a positive effect on early childhood environments. However, the best source for implementing high standards is the early childhood teacher who is willing to continue learning about the elements of quality programs and how these environments positively impact the development of young children.

Inspecting the Environment

To maintain high standards, it is essential to establish a consistent cycle of environmental evaluation. This strategy can have a positive impact on all aspects of the program. Take steps to ensure that all participants are involved in the process. Encourage them to communicate their concerns and wishes, so the inspection will be helpful. As teams of teachers work together to evaluate their environment, equipment, and materials, they will maintain and change the quality of the classrooms.

Aesthetics

Aesthetics, which involves the senses, refers to the overall appearance of the childcare environment. How does the setting smell and sound? Does it convey a positive image? How do people feel when working and playing in the childcare environment? Is this an interesting place to be? Is it beautiful? Does it contain unique features that capture the children's interest and imagination?

Why should you be concerned with beauty in an environment for young children? Because beautiful spaces, like beautiful things, inspire us, make us feel happy, and nurture our creativity. When happy and contented, we are apt to become engaged in interesting projects. We come to value and appreciate the beauty in the world around us.

A Place to Begin: Softening With Pillows

Many surfaces in an early childhood classroom are cold and hard. A simple way to soften the spaces is to add personalized pillows. Bright colors (colours) and creative designs can add life to an old chair, a housekeeping center, or a quiet place. Customize a ready-made pillow or make one of your own. Pillows about 14" x 14" (35 cm x 35 cm) are manageable proportions for the classroom, although other size variations are possible. Make pillow covers using fuzzy fabric, animal prints, iridescent materials, upholstery remnants, canvas, tapestry, woven materials, or scraps of quilting.

Bubble Wrap Pillow

Make a unique pillow from bubble wrap. No sewing required!

1. Cut a piece of bubble wrap 12" x 24" (35 cm x 60 cm).
2. Fold the bubble wrap in half and tape two sides together with clear packing tape.
3. Fill the inside with colorful items such as ribbons, fabric, empty snack bags, scraps of colored paper, colored socks, and so on. There are many colorful possibilities for stuffing.
4. Once the pillow is full, tape the open end together. (Don't over-fill or the seams will split.)

The Library area

chapter 6

Assessing What You Have

Environmental Design Experiences

Many early childhood educators commit time and effort to developing and organizing the various physical spaces in their classrooms. Through this process, teachers influence how the areas function. They determine how spaces are arranged and what they contain and when to rearrange environments and make them inviting for young children. These are important decisions that offer both teacher and child an opportunity to explore the dimensions of color (colour), sounds, textures, light, smells, and objects of interest and beauty.

Children are influenced daily by these environmental decisions. The arrangement and organization of the environment has a tremendous impact upon curriculum choices and the behaviors (behaviours) of young children. Many educators are in tune with this fact and have experienced the powerful influence of the environment.

Examining Three Environments

The First Environment

At the end of an active day, preschool teachers bring into the classroom a "new" selection of materials and small furnishings. Because these items have been stored in a closet filled with boxes and bags, they have been out of sight for some period of time.

The next morning, the children's play is very energetic. They explore the new items that have been, as if by magic, placed in the house-keeping area. The children are busy! Their voices ebb and flow from quiet murmurs to squeals of delight. Teachers stand back and watch. In this environment, frequent changes occur with the addition of "new" materials and furnishings.

The Second Environment

In this early childhood setting, teachers seldom change the environment or materials. Month after month, the activity areas and the materials within these spaces remain the same. The spaces are static; few environmental changes occur. Sometimes, it is because of a lack of available materials. Other times, it is finding the energy to add new elements. The children in these settings are sometimes engaged in classroom activities but every now and again, a burst of restlessness takes over. One child takes a toy from another and a tug-of-war ensues. The children do not appear to be deeply committed to any experience in this place. As the year progresses, children lose interest and become even less engaged.

Another Environment

The programs (programmes) of Reggio Emilia seem to combine the best of the two environments described above—they combine both consistency and use of new materials. In their schools, lively animated children are highly engaged within a "beautiful environment" that they shape. It is also an environment that provides support within a consistent design. The children move freely between activity locations, and they are in deep concentration when engaged in art experiences or long-term projects. This effectively designed environment works well and does not require major changes or frequent experimentation.

North American teachers are often searching for new and helpful strategies to enrich their environmental design efforts. The following sections may be helpful as you add new approaches to your current environmental design portfolio. Perhaps, you will make some new discoveries that you will want to retain for many years.

Travel Along a New Path—Personal, Environmental, and Team Inventories

When changing and improving classroom environments, it is important first to revisit your own understanding of spaces. How do they come about? What personal preferences impact the final design? The intent of the Personal Inventory is to bring teachers to a new level of self-understanding. The goal of this section is to share a number of strategies that are helpful in establishing effective classrooms. This process involves more than acquiring space, selecting materials, and equipping it with child-appropriate furnishings. Doing these things is certainly a first step. But, designing an environment is far more complex and includes the study of many other factors.

Because of time constraints, early childhood training often does not address in-depth issues relating to classroom design. Topics such as evaluating lighting in a classroom, arranging materials, how to paint the walls or display children's work, and many other aspects of the classroom environment are left to experimentation on-the-job. The Personal Inventory provides questions for self-discovery and discussion. It offers a foundation for you to begin the environmental study.

Personal Inventory

Another way to think about classroom spaces is to understand your own personal views about space, and all that is associated with environments. Try this exercise and make some personal discoveries.

Personal Inventory: Your Views About Space

1. Close your eyes and recall a favorite (favourite) setting.
2. What sounds did you like at this place?
3. How about the sense of touch?
4. In what place do you feel the smallest?
5. Where do you feel the largest?
6. Where do you feel alone?
7. Where do you feel the most crowded?
8. Look around your home. What items or features make you feel comfortable?
9. What don't you like?
10. What are some "things of beauty" that you enjoy?
11. What colors do you like?

Scanning the Environment

Another way to awaken your ability to see and appreciate the environment is to conduct an Environment Scan. It is difficult to concentrate on or notice specific aspects of a space when it is filled with children involved in activities. Your attention is focused on the children. To help you focus on the environment complete the Environment Scan for several areas in the classroom. Over time, the seven questions will become so familiar to you that you will be able to ask them without using paper and pencil. Your ability to work directly with the children and still be attentive to environmental issues is increased by this focused observation. (See Appendix C for the Environment Scan form.)

The Environment Scan

Use a separate Environment Scan sheet for each area of the classroom. Include all of the children's activity areas as well as the program support areas, such as the cleanup sink or bathroom. In addition to recording the classroom area and date, you will answer the following questions.

1. What do you see?
2. How do you feel about what you see?
3. What do you like?
4. What don't you like?
5. How does this compare to any of your other experiences?
6. What environmental principles are being applied?
7. What has been discovered?

The Team Inventory

After you have completed the personal and environment scan, it is time to conduct a team inventory. The purpose of this survey is to locate others who share your interest in classroom environment. It will help you identify other teachers who have similar interests, share common skills, and can collaborate on environmental issues. Hopefully, they will contribute to or assist you with a project. Some team members will be able to view your classroom in a new and different way, others will share their ideas, skills, and resources. Still others may be able to sew, build, or create props. Sometimes teachers have expanded their team to include parents and interested community members. These individuals can help identify new possibilities and resources available to use in the classroom. (See Appendix D for a sample Team Inventory form.)

Ways to Review Existing Spaces

Learning to See

When entering a new space, the freshness of the experience enables you to notice many things. After numerous visits, familiarity sets in. Working within the classroom, you may no longer notice many aspects of the space. However, there are strategies and experiences that can help awaken your ability to see the setting again. Select the method that will help you maintain your ability to "see" constructively and imaginatively.

A Photographic Scan

Take photographs of every aspect of the classroom. Pictures offer a precise way to see the features of both small and large areas. Teachers who can no longer see their settings with critical eyes will benefit from

this experience. Photos help identify specific tasks that require your attention and provide a reference for future change. They also record the process of change by providing "before," "during," and "after" photographs.

A teacher and child taking pictures seen in the mirror

Begin by sorting the photos into three categories:

1. "Keep it like it is."
2. "It will be fine, for now."
3. "Needs immediate attention."

After sorting, place the photographs into photo protector pages. Then, put the photos into a three-ring binder with a labeled divider for each category. This will make viewing and reviewing much easier. By regularly reviewing the photographs, busy teachers can maintain focus on the environment. Use these photographs when you create the final plan for action in the next chapter.

Ways to Revisit Your Own Experiences

Visit Other Settings Designed for Children

Visiting spaces designed for children can provide many new opportunities to think about how a space works and the messages it communicates to children. Children's museums, for example, are wonderful places that inspire children to discover and experiment with unique materials. They are often organized into learning areas that contain all the materials and props needed to develop new understanding. The environment clearly communicates that here is a place where children can touch, see, and manipulate the materials.

Visit classrooms and centers (centres) that you have never seen. Seek out programs that are recognized for their beautiful and effective environment. What design efforts have been made in these areas? What techniques have teachers used to organize the environment? In

Outdoor areas provide experiences with nature and friends.

one center, clay sculptures are displayed in the welcoming area. Another center has a hand-made quilt sewn from pieces of fabric contributed by children's families. A teacher in another classroom displays colored paper and markers in clear open containers that show a rainbow of colors. What are the messages communicated in these places?

Visits to other childcare settings are helpful in gaining a better perspective of what the spaces of children can be like. Such visits permit you to determine what elements are appealing. It is a powerful experience to see actual spaces in action.

Sketches of Materials and Environments

Take photographs of the spaces you visit to help you incorporate the ideas into your own classroom. Some settings do not permit visitors to take photographs, however. Teachers with the ability to sketch are at an advantage, but even if your drawing skills are at the novice stage, make sketches anyway. Use a book of blank pages for this task, and encourage yourself to draw. (Remember that these illustrations are for your eyes only.) Making a drawing of the materials and equipment as they appear in an environment is a good way to understand the interplay between furniture, materials, and space. Review and study your drawings often to gain a new perspective and appreciation for spaces. By drawing or sketching these spaces, you will be training your eye to informally measure areas and become more proficient in making good judgments about room arrangements.

Awareness of Place

Up to this point, the focus has been on developing your sense of awareness. Your appreciation for the elements found in the spaces around you will continue to grow; however, you need to nurture it. For example, some of the information you collect for your design files may represent settings outside the realm of the children's world. The benefit of the collections is to extend your ability to identify what you can creatively generate in your space. It may help you use the materials in your classroom in new and innovative ways.

An Inventory of Environmental Tools

There are several formal instruments and informal techniques that you can use to study the environment. These tools provide another way to take a closer look at the space for young children.

Professional Tools for Environmental Study

Teachers can elect to use professional tools intended to assist them in determining the quality of their environments.

The Early Childhood Environmental Rating Scale (ECERS) is an evaluative tool that has been used for some time to determine the quality of an early childhood classroom. The observer responds to a series of categories that reflect most of the activity and physical space components found in programs for young children. ECERS uses a seven-point rating scale and addresses 32 elements. A teacher or evaluator can tabulate their responses and record the results on a graph, which immediately reveals the classroom's profile on the environmental scale.

Harms, Clifford, and Cryer have also developed rating scales for school-age, infant/toddler, and family childcare environments. Each of these scales provides staff with information that is helpful in identifying areas of strength and need in these specific settings and in evaluating environments that serve young children.

The Guide to Accreditation, published by the National Association for the Education of Young Children, includes some criterion for evaluating the physical environment of early childhood programs. Their rationale is: "The physical environment affects the behavior and development of the people, both children and adults, who live and work in it." It further states that the quality of the space and materials influences both the level of involvement and quality of interactions between children and adults in the environment. The self-study and validation visits can provide additional opportunities and specific guidelines for looking at the physical environment of the program.

Informal Tools

The relationship between space, materials, equipment, and children's activities is a delicate balance. Making lists is an easy way to determine how a setting within a room is responding to the program's expectations. The format requires teachers to record only what they see, so it is easy to use. In addition, this process can be integrated with the program's inventory requirements, if such demands exist. (See Appendix E for Space—Materials/Equipment—Activities Profile form.) This form is an excellent tool for evaluating a program's space, materials/equipment, and activities.

As the teacher, you are the designer of your classroom space. Every teacher has unique interests and personal preferences that influence each classroom environment. Although space and materials already exist in a classroom, it has the potential to become a beautiful place filled with appropriately designed areas and thoughtfully created displays.

A Place to Begin: Museum or Art Gallery

Plan a field trip for yourself. Visit a children's museum, art gallery, or Children's Hospital. In this "new" environment, observe how color, lighting, texture, and display are used to create interest and beauty. Notice the placement of the pictures, the open space, and the organization of the place. How can you transfer this design to the place where you and your children live?

The Science area

chapter 7

Making a Plan that Works for You

Designing Your Classroom Space

You are now ready to design a plan for your classroom. The following simple procedures will help you begin to study and work with your space in a planned way. This systematic approach will assist you in identifying the elements that work and those that you can change to make the area more effective for young children and busy adults. You have the power to positively influence the environment where you and the children live each day. This plan will help you in the process.

What Happens in This Place?

The early childhood classroom centers around the needs of active and imaginative young children. Here, children can move around the space, make personal choices, and return to the places they like best. The environment provides support for their need to explore and to develop independence. It includes places for privacy and individual work, as well as for meaningful stimulation and calmness.

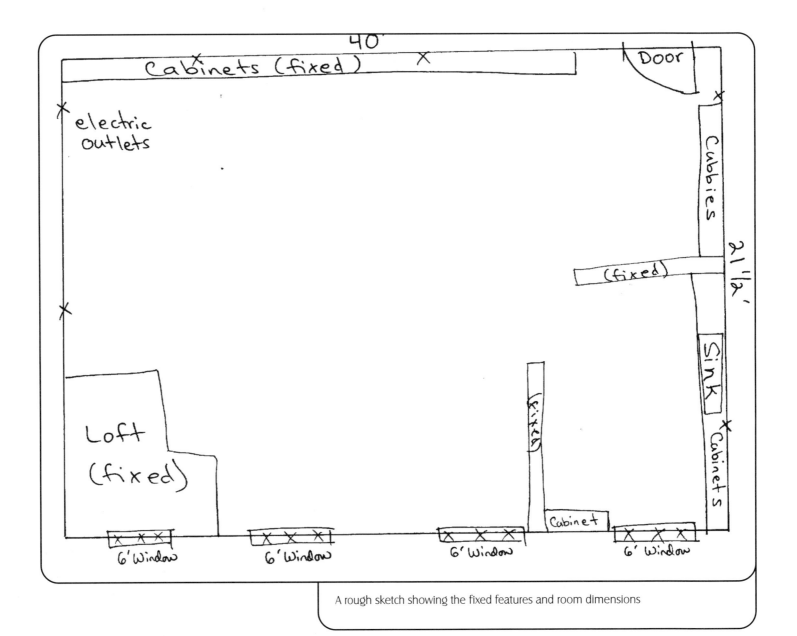

A rough sketch showing the fixed features and room dimensions

The well-designed classroom has activity areas, including messy/wet, quiet/passive, dry/tidy, and active/noisy, and places for small groups, large groups, and individuals to work. It has storage that allows young children easy access to materials, and display areas to provide encouragement and personal pride by featuring the work of children, completed or still in process.

A Professional Look at the Classroom

As you begin the process of designing your classroom, you will need to collect some tools, including a pencil, art eraser, ruler, ¼" (6 mm) graph paper, and measuring tape.

A Drawing of the Classroom

Make a rough drawing of your classroom. In your drawing, include all the fixed features—the items that cannot be moved. These fixed features include windows, doors, bathroom areas, sinks/cabinets (cupboards), counters, electrical outlets, and storage units that are securely attached to the wall or floor. Be sure to check all the enormous bookcases and storage units to determine if they are permanently affixed. Sometimes, we assume that a large storage unit in the middle of a wall is attached. Because the unit has always been in this place, we have come to believe that it cannot be moved. However, a closer look at the bookcase may reveal that it is really not a fixed feature but simply a very heavy unit that is mounted to the floor and wall with removable attachment devices.

Your rough drawing or sketch will give you a better understanding of the actual workable space within the classroom. It will also help you identify the elements that you cannot change and, therefore, have an impact on how space is used.

Measuring the Room

Take measurements of the entire classroom space. Remember to include the "real" fixed features too, such as a bookcase or heavy storage unit. Where is the entrance to the classroom? Is there another exit? Where are the windows and counter spaces? Include these in your drawing. Record the measurements for the entire room, including the walls, windows, doors, and other non-moveable features, and transfer the information to the rough sketch or drawing. Double-check your measurements so that your next step—drawing on graph paper—will be accurate.

The Classroom on Graph Paper

Your rough drawing and measurements will assist you in completing a floor plan that is to scale. With accurate proportions, all who view it can understand it. Using graph paper composed of ¼" (6 mm) squares, make a scale drawing that is ¼" (6 mm) to 1' (30 cm). This means that each square represents one foot. Using a ruler that is clearly marked in ¼" (6 mm) increments will assist you as you transfer the rough drawing and measurements to the graph paper. This drawing will allow you to represent the classroom on a manageable piece of paper. Later, you can use this floor plan to arrange and rearrange the moveable features: tables, chairs, small moveable shelves, and activity areas. (Graph paper is included at the end of the Appendix on page 162.)

It is useful to make several copies of the scaled floor plan. You can use them to create different options. Another way to create multiple

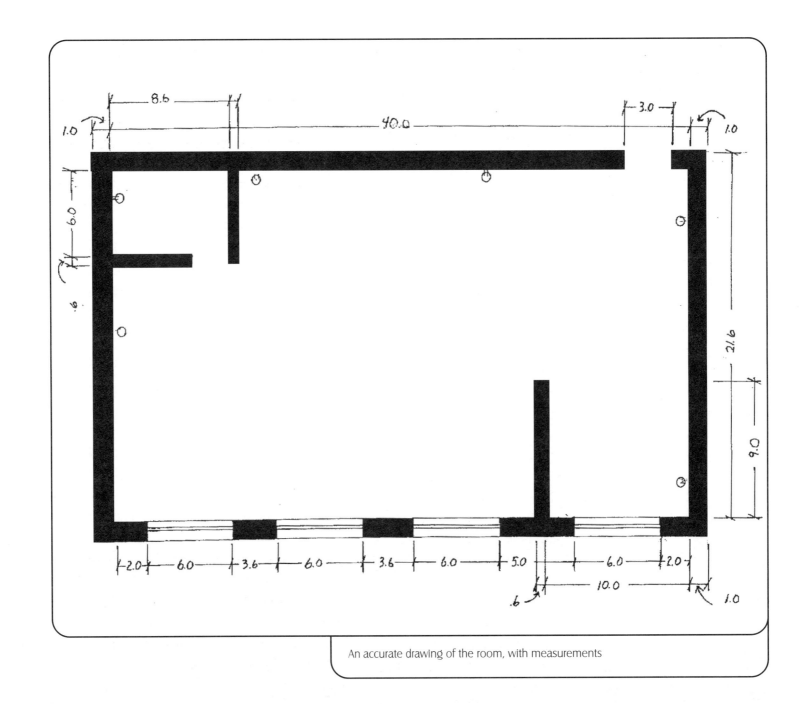

An accurate drawing of the room, with measurements

options is to place translucent tracing paper over your original diagram. The translucency of the paper allows you to make a series of room arrangement variations.

This accurate drawing becomes the basic document to use as you study your classroom space. It will allow you to move furniture and activity areas without physically changing anything until you are satisfied with the layout and are ready to make actual changes.

Drawing

Begin drawing your dimensions on the graph paper by placing the longest walls on the paper first. Use a ruler to help you translate the actual 1' (30 cm) measurements to ¼" (6 mm) squares. (If you are using another paper scale, make the appropriate adjustments.) You will use the same ratio throughout your plan and, even later, when you add the furniture. Transfer the windows, doors, and other fixed features in the rough plan onto the graph paper. It is also important to mark the placement of electrical outlets, heating/cooling units, and other similar fixed items. Be sure to indicate tiled and carpeted areas, as this will influence the type of activity that occurs in these spaces. Use a soft lead pencil and art gum eraser as you begin to represent your classroom space on paper. If you have never used graph paper, this may be a slow process. But as you begin to understand the system, you will be able to complete the drawing easily. It is important to use graph paper because it helps insure that the dimensions are accurate and carefully represented.

This drawing is an essential tool in the design process because it helps you get a "bird's eye" view of your space. When you are in the classroom every day, you tend to see it from your perspective. This floor plan helps you move beyond your mind set.

Furniture and Movable Units

Take accurate measurements of furniture and storage units in the classroom. Measure the largest width and depth of each piece, which is usually around the base. Draw these dimensions on another sheet of graph paper. Remember to use the same scale as with the floor plan, ¼" (6 mm) to 1' (30 cm). Next, transfer these shapes onto dark construction paper so you can easily see them on the floor plan. Include all items: bookracks, tables and chairs, floor cushions, the kitchen sink, and the science table.

Place these pieces on the floor plan to represent your current room arrangement. This visual representation will help you see the placement of activity areas as well as the pathways.

Taking Photographs of the Classroom

Photographs of the classroom space provide another way to see how the space really looks and works. Take pictures of the entrance to the classroom, the activity areas, the eating/table areas, storage areas, bathroom, and sink area. Photograph all areas in the classroom that the children use. It is very insightful to take some photographs from the children's eye level to help you see how the space looks to them.

The camera shows a true image—not how we imagine it looks. Your photograph collection is a vital source of information that will help you answer the question, "Is this how it really looks?" Later, your collection of photographs will be a valuable reference point to document the changes you made. Before and after pictures help you progress in your thinking and offer a detailed view of what you have created in the "improved" environment.

The graph drawing and photographs provide new insight into your classroom space. The graphed image gives you a picture of available space, exits, and fixed features, and the construction paper furniture units show how the arranged environment currently exists. Photos show how the room actually looks and depicts the way you have displayed and arranged the materials.

Evaluate the Current Environment

From all of the evidence you have collected, begin to evaluate your classroom environment.

1. Can you tell what is valued in this classroom?
2. What kinds of activities go on in this space?
3. Are there varying levels of stimulation?
4. Is the classroom inviting and comfortable?
5. Are similar areas and materials grouped together?
6. Are materials easily accessible to children and activities?
7. How do the classroom photographs make you feel?

Anita Olds, a design expert, concludes that a child's ability to work productively in a classroom is influenced by three factors. These three factors can provide clear direction for looking at the classroom space with a critical eye.

1. The number and variety of things there are to do.
2. The number and variety of places to do them.
3. The organization and accessibility of those things within the classroom space (Olds, 1982, p. 18).

Placement of Activity Zones

The placement of activity areas within the early childhood classroom has a very powerful impact on the way the environment works. An early childhood classroom should provide a variety of activity areas to encourage individual and small group participation. These different areas, when clearly defined, make the space function better for all the children and adults who live in this classroom. These unique and separate zones communicate clearly what happens in the space, how the materials are to be appropriately used, and the behaviors (behaviours) that are encouraged.

When evaluating your space for young children, consider the following zones:

Entry Zone
Children's Clothing Storage Area
Sign-In
Parent Communications
Welcoming Information (pictures of the children in the classroom)
Teacher's Storage Place (for personal materials that are not for children's use)
Active/Noisy Zone
Housekeeping
Block Center (Centre)
Socio-Dramatic Play Centers (e.g., Grocery or Doctor's Office)
Music/Movement Area
Gross Motor Zone
Quiet/Passive Zone
Sleeping/Resting Area
Library Center

The Dramatic Play area

Small Manipulative Materials

Writing/Communications Area

Messy/Wet Zone

Toilet/Diapering

Feeding/Eating

Water

Sand/Dirt

Art Center

Woodworking

Cooking

Science/Nature Center

Dry/Tidy Zone

Woodworking

Manipulative Items

Group Gathering Place

Large Group Discussion and Small Group Projects

Planning/Reflection Space

Group Activity Areas

Puppet Theater (Theatre)

Activity zones contain the space and materials that you will need for work or play to take place. These areas have boundaries or indicators that clearly identify where the activity occurs and what materials are available for use. The size of the activity areas varies, depending on the amount of floor space, the type of experiences, and the number of children using the areas.

Activity areas communicate a feeling that matches the type of experiences that will occur in the space. For example, the library area is well lit and has soft pillows and chairs to use when children "read." Posters, big books, and a variety of children's literature clearly show

that this is a place for enjoying books. The activity areas provide a variety of surfaces on which to work, such as the floor, tabletops, risers, lap trays, small movable platforms, and counters. This allows active young children to move around the space and choose the type of work surface that suit their purpose.

Learning Centers

Many early childhood classrooms include learning centers. These carefully planned spaces allow children to work independently or cooperatively on activities that they have selected. Traditional centers, such as housekeeping, blocks, art, and library, are set up in the classroom for most of the year. However, even though these areas remain in the classroom continually, it is essential to change materials within the centers on a regular basis as the children's interest and discoveries dictate.

Other learning centers rotate into the classroom for short periods of time (two to three weeks). Select centers based on the interests and needs of the children in the program. Examples of changing centers are a grocery store, greenhouse, and camping center. Props and materials that relate to the learning centers provide unique opportunities for expanding the children's play and learning experiences. Often, you can include children in the development of the centers by collecting and building props together. This helps the children understand the changes occurring in the area and value the materials they are using.

Bubble Drawings for the Activity Zones

Using a copy of the floor plan and a clear image in your mind of what activity zones you need, begin to experiment with where to place

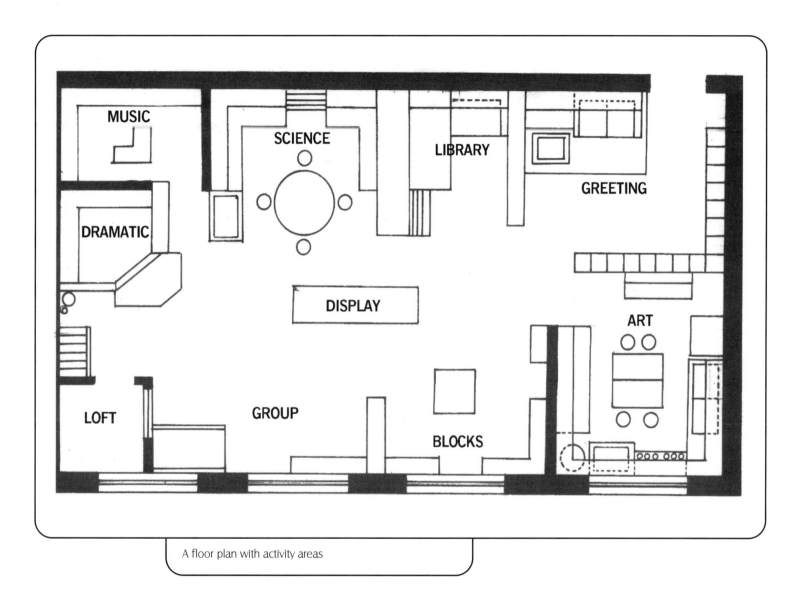

MUSIC

SCIENCE

LIBRARY

GREETING

DRAMATIC

DISPLAY

ART

LOFT

GROUP

BLOCKS

A floor plan with activity areas

zones within the classroom space. Where can you place these zones so they work effectively? Keep in mind that some areas should be close to fixed features. For example, the messy zone should be accessible to the sink or water. The science and nature area might work well near a window with natural light.

Drawing labeled bubbles—creating the zones—on the floor plan enables you to group compatible activities. Grouping similar activity areas together allows less disruption for children working in similar areas or in close proximity. In addition, you can store materials for each zone in appropriate places, close to the activity and easily accessible to young children. When you zone similar activities, children can easily move materials from one space to another without disruption. This permits the integration of ideas and activities as children work within the space.

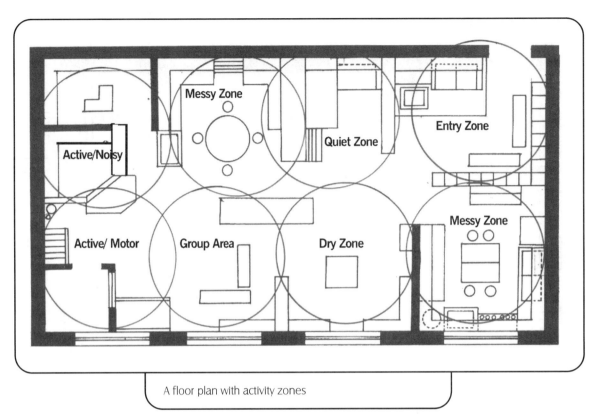

A floor plan with activity zones

Zone Placement

When considering the options for the different activity zones, think about the following:

1. Where will the zone be located?
2. Are there specific needs for the area?
3. What boundaries are needed for visual separation?
4. Are work areas clearly defined?
5. Are there workspace variations: sitting, standing, individual, small group?
6. What storage place for materials is available?
7. Are materials easily accessible?
8. Are materials clearly visible and organized for use?
9. Are a variety of choices available?

Traffic Pattern

Children's movement within the classroom influences the location of certain zones. For example, you should not place the library area near the entrance door or exit area. The housekeeping area works well next to the block area, since children often blend the two and bring materials together in their play. You can make a traffic flow chart, which visually represents the children's pattern of movement during the day. It will help you clearly identify the way spaces work and how the day flows through the activities and routines.

How to Track Movement

Over a two-day period, observe and record the movement of several children and the areas they visit. On a copy of the rough floor plan, make a colored (coloured) line to represent the child you are observing. Where does he enter the room? Where does he go next? What choices does he make and how does he maneuver around the space during the day? To complete the process, record the movement of several children over a couple of days. This will help you identify the children's pattern of movement within the space and the variations that occur.

From your accumulated observation recordings and drawings, compose a master flow chart. This combined traffic flow chart will provide some very interesting data, including how children use the space and move around the area. For example, it will visually show why cubbies do not work in the back of the classroom. How? The chart will show you how

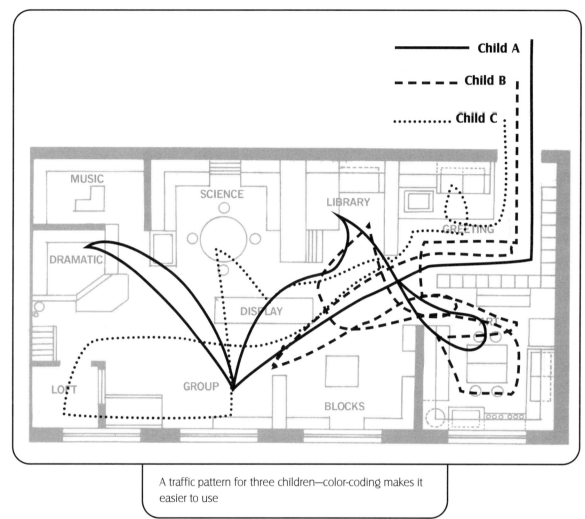

A traffic pattern for three children—color-coding makes it easier to use

many stops the children make when they cross the activity areas to hang up their coat after entering the room. Charting the traffic flow in a classroom is something you should do on a regular basis throughout the year.

Developing a Master Plan: Goals for the Environment

Consider the following questions:
1. What do you want the children to do in the classroom?
2. What are the children interested in doing?
3. What are some of the changes that you want to make to insure these things happen?

List the changes you want to make in your classroom environment. Include the small improvements as well as those that require more work and time. Let the possibilities flow—do not hold back. This is a "wish list," so think big!

Next to each item on the list, place a number to indicate how it fits into your long-term plan. The number 1 indicates an immediate concern that you can complete in a short period of time. The number 2 indicates an area of concern that requires some focused effort, and the number 3 communicates that this item will take longer to complete. For example, relocating the messy areas, such as art and sand/water, closer together might require a minimum amount of work. Since you can accomplish this in one afternoon or a Saturday, place a 1 beside the item. Making small changes and seeing the results of the new, improved environment are good places to begin. Adding a door to the outdoor area, however, may take more planning and work. The door will improve accessibility to the outside, so it will provide positive benefits by extending the learning environment. Record a 3 next to this item on your wish list.

An outside exit from the classroom expands the possibilities for growing plants.

A Plan for My Environment

1. Clean out the storage room. (2) This will take some doing. It would be great to have help.
2. Bring some hardy plants in for the area next to the window. (1) Purchase and place.
3. Re-design the library area: more light, pillows for sitting, tape player and stories, include more books made by the children, and add new books on a regular basis. (2)
4. Build risers to use in the large group area. (3) Definitely need carpentry help. Also, collect lumber and tools. Get carpet donated.
5. Create an attractive display of pictures of the children for the entrance to the room. (1) Have pictures enlarged, make frames for them, and create an attractive design.
6. Inventory the materials that are available and determine items that are needed. (2).

Priorities

This working list helps you develop short-term and long-term elements for your plan. As you review this new list, determine who can accomplish the task. Can you do it alone or do you need to get additional help? What is the timeline for accomplishing these tasks? Both priorities and timeline help you keep the environmental design on-track.

Possible Helpers

Getting others involved in enriching the environment can help build their sense of ownership. Many parents will be interested in working to embellish the classroom space for their child, if they understand the benefits of the project. Parents and extended family are a good source of ideas and materials that will often work to help transform the classroom space. Working together can turn some long-term projects into manageable ones and push up the timeline.

In many areas, there are vocational schools that train people to work in the trades: carpenters, electricians, plumbers, and landscapers. Throughout these programs, students are required to participate in many projects as part of their training. Often, they are willing to build lofts, bookcases, dividers, and other furnishings if you provide the materials. In fact, sometimes they will need to do the building or construction while the children are in the classroom. This provides a special opportunity for children to observe and even participate in the new construction.

A Place to Begin: Beautiful Fabrics

There are many wonderful, inexpensive materials that you can use to add interest to the classroom environment. You can drape, stretch, hang, and attach lengths of fabric to provide visual appeal and softness to the classroom. Use cotton, chiffon, netting, and gauze in display areas or suspend it from the ceiling to provide variations of light and texture. Although solid, neutral colors are the most flexible, beautifully woven textured fabric provides interest and can draw attention to a special area. For example, fabric from families, such as tapestries or handwork, can provide culturally diverse materials to the space. Fabric can both soften and beautify the classroom environment for all who visit or use the space.

Sheer fabric, draped between dowel rods suspended from the ceiling, provides softness to the space.

chapter 8

The Designer's Toolbox

How a Classroom Comes to Life

As teachers and children live and work in a classroom, the space should reflect their many interests and preferences. A classroom should become very individual in its character and appearance.

The uniqueness of the classroom environment is dependent on many different factors. A central factor is the teacher's past experience in room set-up. Time to plan and organize elements within the space is also critical. Over time, the classroom takes on a personality of its own. The existing setting also impacts how you integrate new items into it. For example, new furnishing and materials, purchased or donated, are considered and placed if appropriate. A key factor is that as teachers understand and appreciate the importance of the environment, they begin to create classrooms that are lively and functional.

The classroom's physical arrangement and the availability of play and creative materials convey many important messages. Items that are stored with care and attention suggest that they are valued. Children and adults subtly understand this.

An attractive display that includes utensils for lunch

If the physical features of a space are adorned with accessories, such as wall hangings, pillows, and window treatments, the visual images of that space can be pleasurable. Beautiful settings convey a sense of calm. Such settings offer opportunities to develop an appreciation for aesthetics—how color (colour), shape, form, and texture respond and relate to each other and are appreciated by the viewer. All who visit the classroom will come to understand and respect the organization and arrangement of the space. They will experience how the environment supports the children's daily experiences. When features of the classroom are in harmony with the activities of the day and the people who live in the space, the environment will generate positive feelings.

On the other hand, it is very possible that your classroom will receive many furnishings and materials by donation. Budgets are often stretched, so there is limited opportunity to order specific items needed for the classroom. In addition, there may be little time for classroom design and organization. It may not be possible for you to be attentive to classroom spaces in every way. Each classroom setting is influenced by these limitations, real or perceived. Tight finances require teachers to be innovative and creative with found or constructed items.

First Things First: Clutter Control

No matter what routine you establish to care for the classroom environment, the first step must be to control clutter. Clutter can detract from even the most attractive physical spaces. It emerges slowly and systematically for several reasons. If it is unclear where items belong and time is a premium, clutter is inevitable. Lack of sufficient organization is another cause. When items are not returned to designated places, it prevents the classroom from functioning effectively.

A very cluttered storage area

If clutter is evident in your classroom space, taking a snapshot or two may provide the needed incentive to develop new strategies. Be prepared to work on the unorganized areas slowly. Try to imagine what the space will look like when the clutter has been removed and accept the fact that the battle against clutter is never-ending. But, remember that your classroom is a living environment that includes curious and active children—the space will always have a very lived-in look.

Most teachers are creative spirits. They believe that they will be able to convert collected materials into new treasures for the classroom. This can happen, but it takes time, organization, and workspace.

An Approach to Classroom Clutter

1. Set Goals. Identify how you would like the classroom to appear and why the clutter must disappear.
2. Schedule Time. Scheduling a few minutes over several days will offer a slow pace that allows thoughtful consideration of the task. Progress becomes methodical and rewarding. This "few minutes" method is helpful in establishing a long-term pattern for clutter maintenance.
3. Select a Place to Start. Choose an area that will show immediate results. For example, any area that is small and offers a set of clear action steps will be a satisfying place to begin. Eliminating items that have accumulated on top of a storage unit would be a good place to start.
4. Make Decisions. Review each and every element in the area. Determine the value of each element. Should you save items, give them away, or move them to another part of the room for subsequent use? Should some items be converted to other uses, or do they simply require repair?
5. Group Items Together. This is often how clutter develops in the first place. Store items in close proximity to work areas. Use containers, holders, or shelves for storage and accessibility.
6. Establish an On-Going Management System. Even when clutter has been tamed, it can quickly re-appear. A system of easy-to-use guidelines can alleviate this problem. The following will be helpful:
   a) You won't use it if you don't see it.
   b) Keep things where you need them.
   c) Everything has its place.
   d) Label storage places clearly.
   e) If it has not been used in the two years, it is not likely to be used.

The Vision of Your Classroom

It is important for you to visualize how you want the classroom to look. Revisit your design and accessory files to identify items and displays you would like to include in the classroom. Develop an appreciation for beautiful and natural materials. Think about ways to beautify your classroom. How can you maximize the space? Think of changes as opportunities to involve all who participate in the program—children, parents, and teachers.

Where to Find Classroom Materials and Furnishings

There are a variety of catalogs (catalogues) and supply sources that provide classroom materials and furnishings. Such sources offer a diverse collection of options but often at a high cost. An economical alternative is to seek materials and furnishings from other sources: yard sales, flea markets, parents, and the family storage room. The task is to convert them, if necessary, into useful, attractive, and safe items that are appropriate for children's spaces.

In the Classroom

The first place to begin your search is within your classroom. Very often, you can refurbish and relocate existing furnishings and materials within the room. The results can be surprising! A good example of this is when the teachers in a preschool setting observed that the children had developed a growing interest in playing with the puppet collection. The children's play resulted in elaborate dramatic productions on the surface of a toy shelf. However, this makeshift puppet stage was less than effective. After much discussion and planning, the children and teachers found an unused shelving unit in the storage room, which they promptly converted into a distinctive and colorful puppet theatre. They attached an arch of white plastic pipe to the cabinet's (cupboard's) sides and added a two-part, pull-to-the-side drape to define the platform. This new stage enabled the children to put on dramatic and creative productions. In addition, they found ample space for storing the puppets and props below. Not only did this innovative recycling project save the program many dollars, it also inspired many hours of creative and innovative play for the children.

At Home

Frequently, materials and furnishings found in our homes can become a source of classroom embellishment. For example, you can create a suitable classroom table by reducing the height of a medium-sized adult dining table. Upright storage units originally made for home use can find a meaningful place in a classroom, too. Paint the storage unit and remove the doors to bring new life to it. Another example is leftover kitchen cabinets from a renovation project, which are ideal for the Dramatic Play Center (centre).

Other Sources and Resources

Check flea markets, yard sales, and any other center that recycles home-based materials. They offer many unique items that can add new interest to the classroom.

Innovative Ideas

Teachers and parents can convert collected materials into useful items for the classroom. This refurbishment takes time, organization, and patience, and it helps to have sufficient storage and a workspace. As more teachers begin to tackle the task of enhancing their classrooms, acquiring new skills and knowledge is essential. For example, sawing wood, using an electric drill, and getting familiar with the array of fasteners and glue compounds are skills needed by the do-it-yourself designers in classrooms. The willingness to develop these new skills is an important characteristic for today's early childhood educators. If this is a new prospect for you, the following sections will provide assistance in helping you become an effective designer of your classroom space. In preparing for classroom decoration projects, you must use a number of tools to assist you in your new role.

Storage: A Constant Concern

Storage space is essential for every program. Unfortunately, for reasons that mystify most educators, there never seems to be enough. Many teachers have identified lack of storage as the most persistent problem within classroom spaces. When a new childcare facility is designed, a great deal of time is spent determining the storage needs and finding the appropriate locations. However, the sheer volume of storable materials is always underestimated. And in established classrooms, the problem can be very troublesome. Storage sites always seem to be overflowing, and as donations and new finds arrive, shelving and storage spaces become scarce. Since there is limited time for sorting and re-shelving, the problem grows.

Impact on the Program

Many classrooms have a serious problem. Clutter is everywhere; disorganization reigns. Materials and equipment are inaccessible, so the use of materials is limited. When materials are difficult to find, or you have no time or energy to retrieve them, the variety of materials being integrated into the children's learning experiences is reduced. Lack of storage or poor storage of materials has a tremendous impact on program quality.

Space and Activity Center Differences

Equipment and materials form an important cornerstone of the child's experience. Therefore, it is vital to have suitable and varied storage space. Spaces and activity centers within a program are furnished with **differentiated** materials and equipment. For example, note how different the Housekeeping Center is from the Block Center or the Library Center. Each center needs special materials that often must be stored in unique ways so they are accessible to children during their play.

Principles of Good Storage

It is possible to maintain good storage in a busy classroom or childcare center by following a few steps.

Step One: Assess storage arrangements and needs
- To understand the depth of any storage issue, ask yourself these questions:

- What do you need to store?
- How can you store it best?

Begin by focusing on a specific part of the classroom. Try to answer these questions:
- What happens in this area?
- What items are used in this space?
- Do you have to put away the items so you can use the area for another purpose?
- Are materials near activities?
- Are there sufficient storage places?
- Can children find and return the items?
- Are there any items that adults must retrieve and store?

Once you have answered these questions, you will have a clear picture of the area's materials and storage requirements.

Step Two: Inventory lists

The second step in organizing storage is to develop a list of all the items that are or should be used in an activity area. If you have an updated inventory list, this task is already partially completed. If not, create an item-by-item listing of what is housed within the space and its related storage area. Then, identify other items that would be helpful to have in the area. Add these items to the new or pre-existing lists. Continue to compose lists for the entire classroom. Over time, develop inventory lists for the entire childcare setting. When new materials and equipment arrive or items are no longer available, make these notations on the list. (See Appendix A for sample Inventory Form.)

Step Three: Downsize

Inventory lists are valuable in determining frequently used materials, as well as those that are never used. A good rule-of-thumb is that anything you haven't used within a two-year period, reassess, use, recycle, or give it away. This process will enable you to make existing storage areas available for useful or new items. Remember, more is not always better.

Step Four: Grouping items together

The next step is to group similar items and materials. For example, place all the paper products used for creative activities together. Then, attractively arrange them according to color or size. Storing them in one location can alleviate frustration when you are looking for a particular type of paper product. Another example is to store sand play materials in the indoor sand play area. If you store meaningful sand play items, such as strainers, inside a cabinet far from the activity, they will not be used.

Step Five: Moving from uncluttered to aesthetically pleasing

The final and most dramatic stage is the arrangement of materials within the classroom. By grouping together items and storing them near the appropriate activity, you have increased the potential for their use. Now find ways to attractively arrange the materials, focusing on the visual impact they create. Be inventive. Be creative! Think of how to display materials in different ways. Can you store them in beautiful woven baskets or place them in clear containers that make the contents visible? Could you hang paint tools on a wall using a clear shoe storage unit? Brainstorming with co-workers can often generate new ideas. Develop a "seeing eye" for interesting ways to place objects or to group them together in an attractive way.

Water play with interesting toys and bubbles

Design File: Storage

For innovative ways to organize items in storage units, develop a "clip file" of storage ideas that you like. Add this to your design file (discussed in Chapter 3). Determining what appeals to you will provide a catalyst when confronted with classroom storage issues and the need for beautiful arrangements.

Sufficient and Appropriate Storage

The amount and type of storage in every classroom is unique. Each classroom's environment and activity areas vary, and so does its storage arrangements and capacity. Appropriate storage also depends on the ages and abilities of the children in the classroom. In addition, adult likes, dislikes, and attention to detail will affect the features and characteristics of the storage design.

Safety

Regardless of the type or quantity of storage arrangements, whether for children or adults, they must be sturdy and safe. Place heavy items into containers made of durable materials, such as wood or firm plastic. Store lighter items in less durable units, such as cardboard boxes or baskets. It is critical, however, to make sure the size of the storage shelf is suited to the size of the container. Protruding items on a shallow shelving unit present a potential problem. Always consider how children will retrieve and return items. Store heavy, bulky items at low levels and lighter, smaller items on higher shelves.

Types of Storage

Open Storage is primarily associated with placing assorted materials for self-selection and immediate use. Teachers often set up this type of storage in areas used by children. The arrangement of play items and activity materials is inviting and conveys a hands-on message. In addition, using containers that are well suited to their contents assist children in selecting items and returning them to the storage shelf.

For adults, open storage is usually confined to the storage room or closet. Recently, however, teachers have begun to develop aesthetic storage spaces within the classroom. For example, you can tastefully store items that are not currently in use on open shelves in clear containers. Pay special attention to how you group materials and arrange the items. The items that you place on open shelves should be

Open storage that is attractively arranged

frequently used or have decorative qualities. These decorative items have a curriculum connection and provide an insight into the culture of the classroom.

The teachers and parents in one toddler classroom collected a large number of baskets and containers made of natural materials, such as bamboo, reed, and grass, which they used to store play materials. The children were so interested in the containers, the teachers began to collect other items made of similar materials. The collection included boxes with and without lids; trays (circular and rectangular); tall and short baskets; and small, medium, and large storage units. (The addition of a small set of reed nesting boxes proved to be a real treasure for the children.)

Closed Storage occurs behind cabinet doors or within drawers. Functionality is the primary concern for this type of storage. You must be able to retrieve and return items easily. Therefore, clear and precise labeling is essential. Without labeling, you are likely to overlook or misplace items, and you may lose valuable storage space. Posting inventory lists on cabinet doors and drawers helps with item use and restocking.

Drawers present a common problem—there is a tendency to over-fill them. When this happens, the drawers become too heavy to maneuver and difficult to organize. Keep drawers no more than ¾ full at all times. Organize drawers using small containers or baskets to hold small items. You can make organizers by gluing or stapling long strips of cardboard or thin plastic to create organizational spaces for small items. Since drawers are very difficult for young children to use and provide poor accessibility, they are primarily for adult use. Apply furniture polish or candle wax to the drawer runners to keep them opening and closing smoothly.

A corner unit, attached to the wall, provides interesting storage for work in progress.

Fixed Storage represents any storage unit that is secured to the wall. An example would be a large, one-piece unit that has been positioned after much thought and planning. Another form of fixed storage involves shelving material resting on shelf support systems that are attached to the wall. This type of storage is flexible and meets the varied needs of children.

Adjustable Storage has the flexibility often needed in early childhood classrooms. You can change this type of storage to meet the shelving space requirements of various materials. Modern technology has also generated prefabricated brackets in a variety of sizes and finishes. Some secure to the wall, while others are mounted on metal uprights that have notched ends on the bracket.

Some cabinets have four sets of drilled holes to hold plastic or metal support studs for shelf panels. These are easy to adjust. The task involves estimating the required number of shelves and positioning the supports in the proper place to insure level shelf surfaces.

Portable Storage units are very functional. Portable storage units can be easily moved to any part of the classroom. Virtually any container of any size that can be carried with ease fits this storage category. Boxes, baskets, and bins are the major forms of portable storage used in classroom spaces. These can vary in size, shape, texture, and color.

Choose portable storage units to hold specific items. Place single storage units or clusters of the same type on either open or closed shelves. Clusters of similar portable units generate an impressive and aesthetic arrangement. Where you place them depends on the availability of open shelving and how frequently the contents are used.

Portable storage

Shelving Materials and Support

Shelving is usually made from pine or cut to size from plywood. (Always use boards that are at least ¾″ (2 cm) thick.) Other materials include plastic-coated shelving materials, which are long-lasting and come in a variety of finishes. Another material is reinforced glass. It is attractive when you light it for display purposes, but it is expensive.

Make sure there is an optimum span between shelf support brackets. If using the shelf to hold heavy materials, then make the distance between shelf supports small. You can place lighter materials on shelving that has a greater span between supports. The type of material and thickness of the shelving board will determine the optimum span. (See Appendix F for more information about wall fastenings, support systems, and support span distances.)

Attaching Shelves to Walls

It is possible to attach shelves to most surfaces. Before selecting the wall fastener, inspect the wall. Exterior walls can be made of brick, block, or studs and gypsum board. Interior walls can also be made of brick or concrete block, but most are constructed with wooden studs and gypsum board. It is important to match the type of wall surface to the most efficient securing hardware fastener. It is important to place fasteners into solid materials, such as brick, block, or wood. Secure fixed shelving supports to the wall with screws or Ardoc (screw-like shank) finishing nails. Adjusting fixed shelves is a complicated task that involves removing fasteners and repairing the wall surface.

Getting the Job Done

You have determined that you can improve storage in your classroom, and you are convinced that new arrangements will expand the available workspace. So far, you have reviewed the inventory lists and noted what new items you might acquire in the near future, sorted and categorized equipment and materials, and selected storage sites and designs. A lot of thinking and planning has taken place!

Posted Reminders

You now have a plan for improving classroom storage. Post your plan in a visible location in the classroom. For example, a good place to post small drawings of the project is near the sink where you wash your hands. Posted timelines are also helpful reminders for anyone with a busy schedule.

While it is important to have an overall plan, be prepared to accomplish the work in stages. Mark off the tasks as soon as you complete them. This will serve as a small but important bit of positive encouragement to help you move on to the next step in organizing the storage. (See Appendix G for useful Storage Ideas.)

The Designer's Toolbox

In today's classroom, a new collection should be included in the teacher's professional materials—a box of tools. Teachers in early childhood education programs who are interested in developing classroom materials need tools. Tools are essential for any project. Your toolbox should hold a range of items, from a simple hammer to a sophisticated, cordless, rechargeable, electric screwdriver. The development of many electrically-driven tools, such as the electric

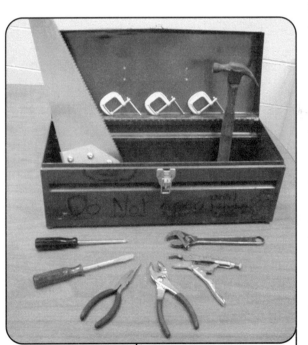

Basic tools

staple gun, make building projects easier and less dependent on physical strength.

Basic Tools

Clamps. When you need to repair items with glue, using clamps ensures that the parts will adhere properly. Smaller C-clamps are ideal for holding work areas steady when you cut or drill. Longer, adjustable bar-clamps are best for tasks such as the clamping process required when you repair sprung drawer panels or cracked doors. Remember to protect the surface with small blocks of wood when using clamps.

Hammers. Usually, the claw or carpenter hammer is the most basic tool. It is used for driving in nails, and its split claw end is helpful in removing nails. Hammers come in a variety of weights. The correct weight for you will feel neither too heavy nor too light. Also, consider the length of the hammer when making your selection. For example, a small pin hammer is a lightweight tool with two surfaces, one smaller than the other to sink small nails or decorative tacks. The mark of a good hammer is in its balance and stability. To achieve the maximum force of the hammer, swing it from the elbow rather than the wrist.

Nails. Nails are identified by their length, diameter, and appearance of their heads. Common nails have flat heads that do not penetrate wooden surfaces. Casing nails, finishing nails, and common brads, however, have small compact heads and can easily penetrate below the surface of the wood. Each nail type is used for a particular job. Some nails are designated as "penny" size, particularly when purchased in bulk boxes. "Penny" was originally a measure used in Britain a long time ago. It referred to the weight of the nails per hundred nails and their cost. Today, it simply designates the size and length of a nail.

Another type of nail is referred to as a two-penny nail. Other nails have a spiral or angular (screw-like) shank, which provide greater holding power. Cut brads and cut nails have shanks that are flat, rather than round. In addition, other nails are designed for specific purposes, such as masonry or roofing. (See Appendix H for nail information.)

Pliers and Wrenches. These tools come in a variety of sizes and shapes. Pliers can be either blunt-nosed or needle-pointed and are excellent for pulling nails or hooks out of wood. A wrench looks very much like a member of the pliers' family, except it opens on the side instead of on the top (like pliers). Their uniqueness is enhanced by their ability to adjust and remain securely attached to a nut or other working surface. Another tool is a vice grip, which has an adjusting screw-like mechanism in its handle that secures the tool's jaws. This is an excellent tool for opening white glue jugs when the lids have become difficult to open.

Saws. Once you have a hammer, screwdriver, wrench, and pliers as staple elements in your toolbox, the next tool you need is a saw. Unless you have received sufficient instruction and guidance in using an electrical saw, it is probably not the best tool to choose. Instead, select an all-purpose ripsaw. This saw has a longer blade and good-size teeth for quick cutting. You will find sawing much easier if you apply a drop of oil to the blade. When making small woodcuts, it may be easier to use a smaller miter (mitre) box saw. This saw is used with a miter (mitre) box and allows for 45-degree angle cuts. Another type of saw is a hacksaw, which is ideal for cutting metal. Keep in mind that with guidance, you can add an electric saw to your tool collection.

Screwdrivers. If teachers could use one screwdriver for all of the necessary screwdriver tasks, they would be very happy. This is not the case, however. Screws have specific and unique heads. The Phillips screwdriver, for example, fits the cross-designed, slot head of a Phillips screw. The regular screwdriver fits all single-slot screws. Screwdrivers come in a variety of sizes, to match the size and weight of the screw. Fortunately, there are screwdrivers that make the task of using screws less taxing. The manual type is equipped with an automatic retractor mechanism, which enables you to use less force and rotation to achieve the task. The electric rechargeable version makes the task even easier.

Screws. Screws provide better holding power than nails, and brass and stainless steel screws do not corrode. Their threaded shank grips wood. Screws are best known for their purpose, such as a sheet metal screw, gypsum wallboard screw, deck screw, machine screw, and self-tapping screw. Choose screws for the type of head they have (flat, rounded, pan-head, or oval). Screws also have head features to receive an appropriate tool—either a Phillips or regular screwdriver. (The hex-socket (six-sided) screw requires an Allen wrench to drive it into wood.)

An Organizer Box

Nails, screws, bolts, and nuts are ideally stored in a multi-compartment box. This keeps the various fasteners separated and easy to select.

Additional Tools for the Collector

Electric Drill. The electric drill is the ultimate of tools. Because of its versatility, it is frequently used in building projects. In addition to drilling holes, you can fit it with accessories to mix paint, polish wood, and

An organizer box is useful to keep things sorted

Additional tools

drive in nails, screws, and nuts. Electric drills also come with additional features such as variable and reversible speeds, a feature that is useful for removing screws. One type of drill is a countersink drill bit, which enables you to drill a hole that permits the head of a screw to sink below the surface of the wood.

Fasteners. There are a variety of fasteners on the market to attach things to a wall. Attach items to a sheetrock wall by drilling a hole with an electric drill, then insert a lag screw into the hole. When the screw is secure, the plastic or metal insert expands and holds the fastener tightly in the wall. If the wall is made of cement block, use a cement drill bit with your electric drill to create the hole and insert the lag screw. To be prepared for all kinds of attachments, you need multi-purpose drill bits for drilling wood, block, and metal. A cement drill bit is needed to prepare holes in a block wall. An assortment of lag screws, with inserts, allows you to securely attach a variety of materials to walls.

Use screws, picture hooks, or wall adhesive to attach Plexiglas panels to walls, providing places to display children's pictures, documentation, and information. These panels should be located where young eyes can enjoy the display and even touch the items. Corkboard, fabric-covered panels, and washable white boards provide additional areas for display. Securely attach these to the wall, so they will not have to be re-attached later.

Iron. A steam/dry iron is essential when you are working with fabric. Follow the manufacturer's instructions carefully. You can use an iron for a variety of purposes, including removing the wrinkles from paper and attaching fabric to a wall hanging.

Knives. A craft knife has a plastic or metal handle that is designed to fit snuggly in the hand. It has breakaway blades and is intended for cardboard, paper, and plastic. A slimmer model is a scalpel, which also has a breakaway blade feature and is intended for lighter projects. When using a knife, you will need to use a self-healing mat to prevent rapid dulling of the blade. In addition, it is essential to replace the blade frequently to maintain clean, crisp-cut edges. An excellent tool for cutting or scoring thick cardboard is a marking knife, which is frequently used to mark lumber before it is cut. It has a metal-encased, long blade. When the blade becomes dull, open the metal case and replace the dull blade.

Tape Measure. When working with lumber or measuring the features of a room, a pull-out steel tape measure is invaluable. They can be obtained in various lengths—12' or 25' or meter (metre) tape measures are also available. For smaller measurement tasks, use metal or wooden rulers. Square up your measurement by using a carpenter's (framing) square or a drawing square. An Omnigrid ruler is a clear ruler with black and yellow markings. It is about 2 ½ times as wide as the average ruler. It is ideal for working on surfaces that are light or dark. A common saying heard among carpenters in Canada is, "Measure. Measure again. And measure yet again." In the United States, one hears, "Measure twice, cut once." Both sayings indicate the importance of measuring and re-measuring.

Scissors. Maintain a collection of scissors for specific purposes. For example, use fabric scissors with fabric only. Fabric scissors should be very sharp. Never cut paper with fabric scissors or they will become useless very quickly. Also, consider sharpening them periodically. Embroidery scissors are ideal for clipping threads, cutting small designs, or cutting out small areas within a design. Another type of scissors is a rotary cutter, which is ideal for cutting but requires a cutting mat. Keep a pair of scissors exclusively for paper cutting and label them for this purpose. This will ensure their longevity.

Staple Gun. Invest in two types of stapling tools: the hand-held model and the electric model. The hand-held model is adequate for small jobs, but the electric staple gun is a better choice for large projects. The electric model consistently delivers the staple so it is always tight and snug.

Purchasing Lumber

Wood is a natural product. It is far from perfect and reflects many inconsistencies. It is not always smooth or straight, and may even be cracked (which is called a check). The lumber may appear very unattractive and not be square. (This occurs due to the curvature of the tree). However, a piece of lumber is very valuable and useful.

Selecting lumber for a project should depend on how you will use it and where you will place it. It is critical to make a list of the actual lengths of lumber required for the project. Lumber comes in particular lengths, so if you can determine the best lengths you need, you will eliminate waste. The staff at a building supply store can be very helpful in recommending the most economical purchase. In fact, many will actually cut the lumber to the dimensions you need.

Types of Wood (Note: The numbers indicate hardness—#1 is the hardest; the best-looking grade is Prime.)
#1 Oak—Tan to reddish-brown. Open grain.
#2 Maple—Light in color with a hint of gold. Subdued grain.
#3 Douglas Fir—Almost white with a reddish-brown grain. Gradually darkens to a reddish-brown.
#4 Yellow Pine—Almost white when first cut but turns to a golden yellow. Ranges from clear to knotty grain. Used for load bearing.
#5 Spruce White Pine—Almost white when cut and remains white. It has a subdued grain. Used more for decorative purposes.
#6 Cedar—Varies from light- to mid-brown. Straight grain. Strong scent.

Lumber Sizes

A piece of lumber available as a 1" x 6" (2 cm x 15 cm) product at the building center is, in fact, not that size at all. It is actually ¾" x 5 ½". The following chart will help you understand the difference between the nominal sizes and the actual sizes of lumber in the marketplace.

Nominal	Actual
(Rough sawn, when green)	(Dried, planed, smooth)
1" x 2"	¾" x 1 ½"
1" x 3"	¾" x 2 ½"
1" x 4"	¾" x 3 ½"
1" x 5"	¾" x 4 ½"
1" x 6"	¾" x 5 ½"

This gives you an idea of how different the dimensions of a piece of lumber will be from the time it is originally milled to when it is made available at a building supply center. It is another measurement for you to take into consideration when preparing for a project.

Other Lumber Sources

Check to see if your community offers a demolition materials outlet, recycling center, or salvage store. Recycled lumber can be just as sturdy as new lengths and are much less expensive. Your choice will depend on the nature of your building project. Identify local building sites and visit them. Inquire about their scrap lumber. Ask them what happens to the wood lengths and plywood panels? Often, these scrap pieces are burned or hauled away. You can use these no-cost pieces in many classroom-building projects.

Sanding

It is one thing to build a wooden project, but it is another to give it a finish. Sanding is part of a process to bring the project into its final state. Sandpaper is not made from sand, but is actually coated with metal, crushed rock, synthetics, and ceramics. It ranges from coarse to fine. Coarse grit papers are identified with smaller numbers while the finer papers have higher numbers. There are also other sanding products available. Sanding pads and abrasive sponges are substantial in size and do not require you to use a block. Steel wool is another product that comes in a variety of grades, from fine to coarse. You can use some sanding products wet or dry.

To begin sanding, use coarse sanding products and gradually move to a level of fine papers or fine steel wool. Since sanding produces a fine dust, you should wear a facemask and sand in a room with good ventilation.

Gluing

There are many types of glue on the market. Often, when you think you are using glue, you are more likely using a synthetic adhesive. True glues are made from natural products. Usually, it is bookbinders, conservationists, and possibly some cabinetmakers, who use real glue. The variety of glues (better known as adhesives) permits you to select the right product for the right gluing task. For example, wood glue works best on projects constructed from lumber or plywood.

Finding Help

So far, you may have completed as many tasks as you feel comfortable doing. This might include major portions of your project. How much you do will depend upon the complexity of your storage plan. If you are comfortable working with the materials and necessary tools, then you may not require much extra help.

However, if your project requires using tools and materials unfamiliar to you, it may be a frightening and unsettling experience. These feelings are true for all educators regardless of their gender. If you wish to explore other possibilities and extend your create spirit, identify a co-worker, parent, or friend to serve as a mentor. As you become more confident, you will be able to complete many projects with minimal assistance.

Building Together

An example: A newly established childcare center determined that the prices for cubbies were too high for their budget. The teachers decided that they could dramatically reduce the expense if they constructed their own version. They measured the designated space, drafted a small sketch with the help of the children, and spent many days reviewing the measurements for accuracy. A teacher visited the local lumber supplier to have the boards cut to their specifications.

Over the next week, the teachers took turns applying the paint primer. One teacher was comfortable using tools, so she and a small group of children marked and pre-drilled holes for the countersink screws. More painting took place during the after-school hours.

When the boards were ready, the teachers brought the boards and bags of screws to school. The children and teachers consulted the diagram to help them piece the cubbies together. Three days later, the unit was resting in its place, waiting for the final attachment to the wall. Now the teachers asked for help and guidance, since they were not familiar with attaching a unit to the wall. Their mentor brought the anchors and demonstrated the technique of secure attachment.

"Do-it-yourself" really means to do as much as you are comfortable doing. If there is something you do not know how to do, you can solve the problem with assistance (just as these resourceful teachers did).

Seek Expert Help, But…

If the task is complex or you have determined that it is not a "do-it-yourself" project, your community may have many carpenters or handy-persons willing to help. Consult a telephone directory, personal acquaintances, and parents to guide you in the right direction. But, it is still important to understand the unit's dimensions and how it is constructed. If you know the nature of shelving material types and their recommended span-widths, you can guide the carpenter to ensure that the unit is specifically designed for use by young children in an activity-oriented classroom.

A Place to Begin: Simple Items to Construct

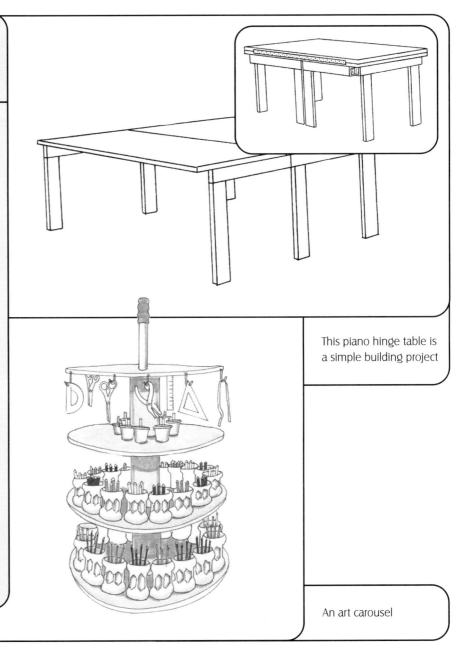

Piano Hinge Table

This simply constructed table can be expanded for use, and then folded to store in a small space.

Directions:

The top of the table is ¾" (2 cm) plywood. Construct the frame using 2 "x 4" (5 cm x 10 cm) lumber and attaching it with screws and glue. To connect the top to the frame, use angle brackets. You can fold the top using a piano hinge (available at hardware stores).

This piano hinge table is a simple building project

Art Carousel

Use this rotating storage unit for an attractive way to display art materials or other small items that you might use in other areas of the classroom.

Directions:

The center of the carousel is a cardboard carpet tube. Make circular shelves using ¼" (6 mm) plywood and attach them to the tube using white glue. Place a dowel rod, 1" (2 cm) or larger, through the center of the carpet tube and attach it to the base.

An art carousel

chapter 9

Enriching the Environment

Visual Displays

In an early childhood environment, children need to be able to see and handle displays. Effective displays inspire ideas and additional work by children who have visited the area. As children's work expands, displays should grow to include evidence of the children's beginning efforts and their steps along the way. Make sure to include children's words and their descriptions of their work in the display.

Children build structures, paint pictures, create with clay, weave designs, write stories, and make books. It is important to find effective ways to display these creations so children and adults can see and handle them. This encourages children to examine their own work and to be inspired by the work of others.

Children may work on projects for extended periods of time. Therefore, they need places to store their work so they can revisit projects and expand their ideas. Display work in progress to provide opportunities for them to evaluate their work and build on ideas. It will stimulate their thinking, aesthetic learning, and the sharing of ideas with others. Effective displays help children understand that their work is important and valued in the classroom.

"Surrounded by words describing their thoughts, by their work and by photographs as they create. Children know that their environment belongs to them and they belong to the environment." (Henry Sanoff, Professor of Architecture, 1995)

Two preschoolers admire their project and pictures of their work.

Tools Needed for Creating Displays

Having basic tools in the classroom or center (centre) can help you create effective displays. These tools will make it easier and quicker to develop and construct a gallery.

Essential Tools

Staple gun and staples: Used for attaching heavy materials.

Small stapler: Used for attaching lightweight materials.

Safety pins: Used to attach fabric, rope, and ribbons that are high above the children.

Masking tape: Can be used in many different ways.

Double-sided tape: Used to join two materials together.

Strong nylon or fishing line: Used for suspending materials and tying things together.

Fine wire: Used to support suspended items that are heavy.

Pliers: Used for all kinds of jobs.

Scissors: Large good-quality scissors are used to cut fabric and other materials.

Retractable craft knife: Used to cut small shapes from thick materials.

Steel straight edge: Can be used for cutting a straight line.

Retractable tape measure: Helps in placing and arranging balanced displays.

Variety of adhesives: Those most frequently used are for paper, wood, and fabrics.

Pens/markers, chalk, and pencils: Include both thin- and broad-line instruments.

Additional helpful items: Map pins (with large colored heads), staple remover, pinking shears, and ratchet screwdriver.

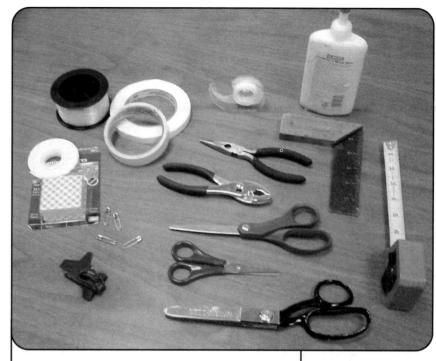

Tools for creating displays

Store these items together (away from children) so they will be available when you need them to create intriguing displays.

Photographs of Work: Documentation

Keep a camera available in the classroom to document completed work and work in progress. Photos provide evidence of the children who worked together and their contributions to a project. They also show the steps in the process, from the beginning to final completion. Children, teachers, and parents can examine and discuss these photographs, again and again.

Children can be involved in the development of documentation panels using these photographs. They can place the pictures in sequential order and provide verbal explanations of what was happening. The combination of language and photographs provides a window to the learning that is occurring as children create and work together. The children, teacher, and community can enjoy an effective display of this documentation.

Photographic Slides

Taking slides of children's work and projects provides another opportunity to explore their creative efforts. These enlarged visuals (shown on the wall or screen) provide a close-up of the integral parts of their work. This large version can provide children with new opportunities for collaboration and revisiting the work for additional extensions. The differences in the images presented on the slides can lead to discussion about the sequence and procedures they used. Young children can use a light table to select and arrange slides for viewing. You can also use the slides in presentations to parents or the community. The slides will provide visual information about the important learning occurring in the program (programme).

A documentation board of the toddler's watermelon exploration

Function of Displays

One of the most important things to consider when creating any display is its function. What is your reason for displaying the items? What do you want others to see? How do these items work together? How can you present it in an attractive manner?

A simple layout works best. It allows each object to be seen clearly or in relation to the companion pieces. Make the background simple as well. It should complement the work being displayed, not overpower or distract from it.

Types of Displays

Informational: Parent notices, center activities, menu, and holiday schedule.

Curriculum: Relates to themes of study, such as a display of science materials, clothing or tools from a culture, or books on a specific topic.

Creative: Natural materials to stimulate language or creative thinking, such as a unique collection of shells or pieces of bark from a variety of trees.

Children's work: Celebrates the learning that has occurred, creative efforts, or project work.

An aesthetically pleasing display for children's work

Two-Dimensional Children's Displays

Develop these displays as children are working on activities or projects. Often, children can participate in creating the layout of photos, drawings, or language. They can arrange their work on paper or the floor, and then discover how it looks when it is well spaced and mounted. These opportunities allow children to experience the visual impact of a design and make personal decisions about the display.

Three-Dimensional Displays

In many early childhood programs, young children make three-dimensional structures, ranging from box structures to wire mobiles. Because some items are fragile, display them so they can be appreciated without manipulation. Sometimes, open shelves can provide the width needed for displaying these three-dimensional works.

Bookcases

Bookcases provide a substantial base for displaying children's larger work. They can also serve as a background for projects. How can you change the bookcases so the focus is on the display of children's work? For example, if the bookcase is bright yellow, it would overshadow anything you display on its shelf. Perhaps you need to repaint the bookcases. Remember that neutral colors (colours) work best as a background for great works of art.

You can provide additional interest to the bookcase by lining the shelves and back with mirrored paper or fabric. (Use solid colors or small patterns so that the background does not distract from the importance of the children's work.)

Some communities have "kiosks," which are displays you can walk around. Transfer this idea to the classroom to provide unique displays. To create a kiosk, staple or glue together large cardboard boxes, then children can paint it or cover it with fabric. To display smaller items, turn boxes (such as shoeboxes) on their sides. This type of display allows children and adults to enjoy their work from many different directions.

Three-dimensional wire sculptures.

Bookcases provide places to display large items created by young children.

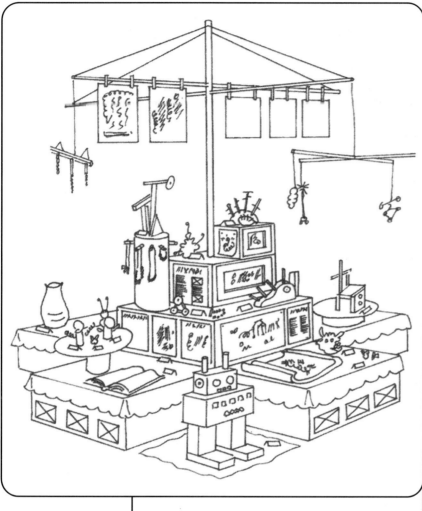

A kiosk for displaying children's work

collection of shells, feathers, or flowers, invite children to discover their qualities, as they float in the air above. String these materials from branches, metal pieces, or heavy wire using yarn or fishing line. It is best to place mobiles where there is air movement, usually near a window, vent, or fan.

A clothesline or pulley system can provide additional display space in the classroom. Suspend the line between two walls, above the heads of adults. Include artwork, portions of projects, or children's photographs on the line. As with all displays, it is best to keep them simple and attractive. Stand back and evaluate the overall look of the space. Do the higher displays make the space more interesting?

Lighting

Special lighting can highlight children's work in the classroom. Most of the lighting in classrooms comes from fluorescent tubes, which is very harsh and broadly distributed. Try to incorporate other sources of light into the classroom. Spotlights are inexpensive and can provide incandescent light to a specific area or display. Floor lamps provide additional light for a tabletop or low display. This local lighting provides pools of light to separate areas and workspaces. For safety, place floor lamps securely behind a display table or cabinet (cupboard) to prevent them from being pulled over.

Strip lighting can also be installed in some classrooms. The strip includes several spotlights that can be turned in different directions to feature special work or displays. Lamps, spotlights, and strip lighting provide a more home-like environment. You can use them to focus on special things to be admired by children and adults.

Hanging Displays

The most unused portion of a classroom is the overhead space. This area can provide new possibilities for displaying attractive items that are visually interesting. Mobiles, constructed from natural items such as a

Working and Sitting Places

Many classrooms are filled with tables and chairs that give children little opportunity for movement. Active young children need different ways to approach their work and focus on a project. Children find it difficult to sit in a chair when they are very excited about an idea. They prefer to work on a surface that is at a comfortable height and allows them to stand or move. There are several different ways to add variations of height to the working spaces in an early childhood classroom.

Carpet-Covered Risers

A riser can provide an appropriate workspace for young children. One or more children can stand and work comfortably around a riser. Risers also allow children to move around their work to see it from another perspective and add additional elements. Risers should be a size so that teachers, but not children, can easily move them. The height of a riser should match a comfortable arm height for the children. (See Appendix I for this information.) You can cover risers with a variety of materials including carpet, upholstery fabric, or absorbent materials. You can also use two or three risers together and place them in different arrangements. For example, an L-shape provides an enclosure for a group area or a boundary for a center. Children can also use risers as a place to present a creative play or musical production.

Lofts

Adding a loft to an early childhood space can increase workspace significantly. The structure also provides many new places for children to collaborate or find a quiet cubby to be alone. The loft, however, must be carefully designed so that it is both safe and functional.

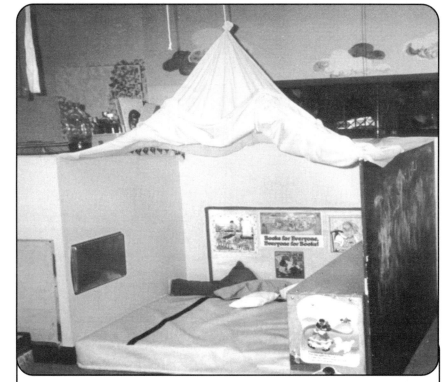

A suspended sheet serves as a canopy for a small space for toddlers to relax and "read."

Questions to ask before you begin construction of the loft:

1. How will the loft be used? Small group, library area, socio-dramatic play, and so on.
2. How will it fit within the rest of the classroom design? Provide new possibilities, expand space in needed areas, and support the curriculum.
3. Is it safe for children and adults? You should be able to observe all areas of the loft and see the children at all times. If there is more than one level, there should be two exits from all levels. The use of Plexiglas has increased the safety of lofts and eliminated the use of railings that could produce unsafe enclosures. Using ramps, rather than steps, makes the structure more accessible to all young children.
4. What is the desired size and shape? For example, if both the upper and lower levels of the loft are children's space, the upper level should be at least 5' (1.5 m) off the floor. If you will be using the lower level for storing materials, the distance can be much less—3' to 4' (about 1 m). Remember, you want these stored materials to be accessible—not forgotten.

The increased height of the upper level of the loft will provide children with a new view of the classroom. Or, perhaps they will now be able to see a window that provides a beautiful view to the outside or see plants that are thriving in the sunlight. Children may use the upper level as a place for working or enjoying books. With proper lighting, the lower level can provide a place for solitude or a quiet activity. The loft's ramp, which leads to the higher level, can offer children a place to experiment with materials by rolling, pushing, or stacking.

There are many possibilities for the use of a loft, but the design should match the needs of the individual classroom and children who live in this space. A carefully designed loft provides visual interest to the classroom, variations of height, and many new work areas for children's activities.

Spool Tables

Another item that can provide an additional work area in the classroom is a low, round table. You can create these tables by using free or inexpensive spools that may be donated by local telephone and cable companies. Because many of these spools have been used for storage outdoors, their surfaces may be very rough. Before adding them to the classroom, be sure to sand the tops and check for rough spots that could be harmful to children. If the table is very rough, glue a piece of linoleum or carpet to the top to provide a smoother workspace.

Mattress

An air-filled mattress can provide an entirely different surface on which to sit, work, or play. You can purchase them in several sizes, but the twin and full mattress probably work best in the limited space of most early childhood classrooms. Or, you can use standard mattresses in infant and toddler's classrooms, as long as you cover the surface with a washable fabric. This soft and raised area gives children a "new" place to relax, hear a story, or simply interact with a friend.

Carpet and Rugs

One of children's favorite (favourite) places to work is the floor. This is a safe place to build a block structure, roll a train, or read a book. To add

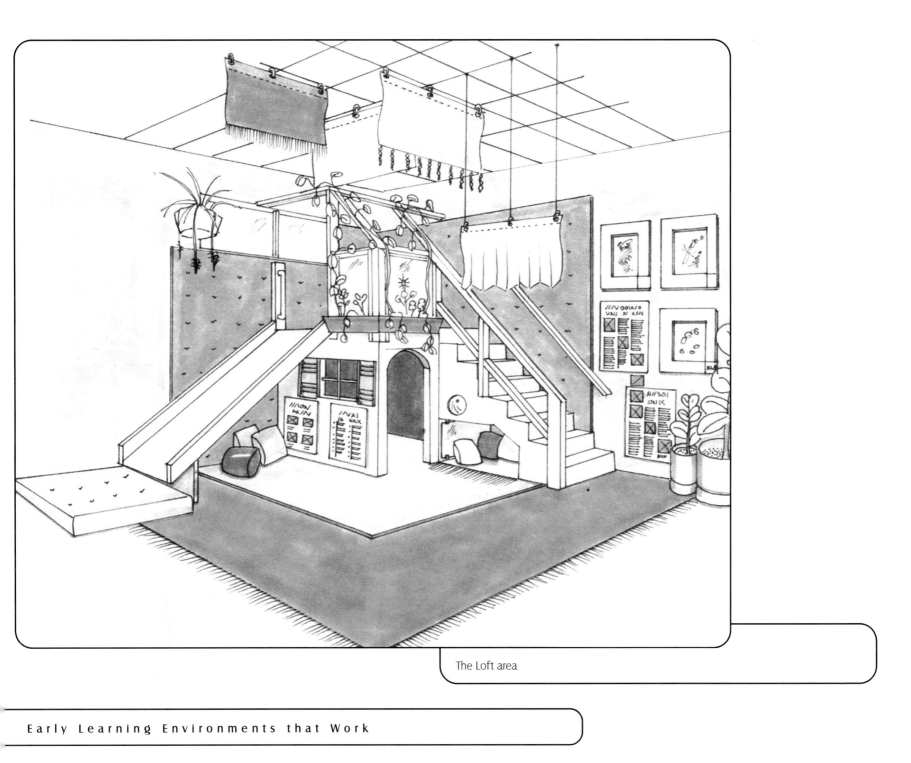

The Loft area

warmth and texture to the workspace, add carpet or area rugs such as washable braided rugs, rubber-backed rugs with designs, carpet samples, or remnants. Choose rugs that are attractive, have an interesting texture, and are safe for walking. You can also mount carpet on walls to increase the absorption of sound or provide an interesting background for a display.

Platform

A platform is a slightly raised area that is securely built so children can work, stand, or perform on the slightly elevated surface. It works best in an enclosed area with limited access. Platforms can inspire performance and dramatic play, as well as provide workspace for large projects. The simplest way to construct a platform is to use 2" x 4" (5 cm x 10 cm) pieces of wood for the frame and ½" plywood that is 4' x 4' in size for the top.

Growing Plants in the Early Childhood Environment

Working to create a more home-like environment for young children and teachers is an important undertaking. One element that adds warmth and softness to a classroom is living plants. There are a number of attractive, hardy plants that can survive in an early childhood classroom with minimal care. These adaptable plants need some light and adjust to both under-watering and over-watering. By caring for plants in the classroom, children develop an understanding of the needs of plants and experience the joy of watching them grow. Green plants provide a nice contrast to the hard surfaces of tile floors and concrete block walls that so often exist in classrooms. They come in a variety of sizes, colors, and textures that add visual interest in the children's space.

Good Plant Possibilities

Boston Ferns, Bird's Nest Fern, Stag Horn Fern. Although you can include all of these ferns in the classroom, some are more readily available in different geographical areas. Ferns need some light and should be kept slightly moist. They also like to be misted on a regular schedule. These ferns vary in texture and shape so they provide an interesting display when grouped together.

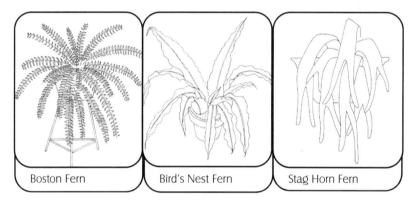

Boston Fern | Bird's Nest Fern | Stag Horn Fern

Corn Plant (dracaena deremensis). A healthy plant that has leaves growing out of a tall, thick stalk. It adjusts to little light as well as little water. The large corn plant can be used to draw attention to special areas in the classroom or provide the foundation for a grouping of plants. (No drawing for this plant.)

Croton (codianeum reidii). This plant can be a colorful addition to the classroom. Their leaves will be more yellow

Croton

and orange if you place them where there is a great deal of light.

Jade Plant (crassula argentea). Interesting plant with succulent green leaves. It needs little water and is a slow grower.

Jade Plant

Norfolk Pine (araucaria heterophylla). This plant looks like an evergreen tree. It has needles and a similar shape to pine trees. It adds an interesting element to the classroom landscape.

Piggyback Plant (tolmiea menziesii). This is a plant that has runners, which provide an easy way to propagate new plants. It works well in a hanging basket or at the base of a large plant.

Norfolk Pine

Rubber Plant (ficus elastica). Attractive, large plant with glossy green leaves. It can grow quite large and have multiple stalks. The variegated rubber plant is more sensitive to environmental changes than the green plant.

Spider Plant (chlorophytum comosum). Robust, hanging plant that has runners that can sprout into little offshoot plants. It is interesting to propagate since the runners root easily in soil or water.

Piggyback Plant

Umbrella Tree (schefflera). This large leaf plant can grow to a very large size. It thrives best with some sun and regular watering.

Wandering Jew (zibrina). This trailing vine has striped leaves that

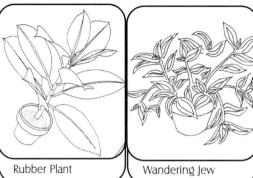
Rubber Plant   Wandering Jew

grow well in a hanging basket. It is easy to propagate in soil or water.

Weeping Fig (ficus benjimina). This very attractive plant has a tree-like appearance. Some varieties have small, green, waxy leaves while others have variegated leaves. The weeping fig can grow quite large and can be an impressive feature in a classroom.

Spider Plant

Plant Display

Grouping together plants that vary in size and form can have a tremendous impact on the appearance of the classroom space. Different size plants that are grouped together provide another opportunity to observe contrasts and add visual interest. (Include variations in the texture and color of plants to add interest to the display.) Plants that are grouped together often seem to grow better. They enjoy the shared moisture in the grouping and aren't forgotten when watering occurs. In addition, plant containers also add aesthetic interest to the area. Sometimes the plant containers are the focus of interest. Other times, the plants are so interesting that simple containers work best.

Umbrella Tree

A plant rack that is easy to make

Although you can display plants throughout the classroom, you can also organize a special place for plants and tools.

An Easy-to-Make Plant Rack

Features of a plant rack:

Child-height working area

Frame made of white or black plumbing pipe and jointers (PVC)

Shelves made of grill-type, plastic-covered metal (the type used for closet storage)

Storage boxes or crates on the floor hold the watering can, mister, plant tool set, and soil/compost for transplanting

A place to hang gloves and gardener's apron

A place for cleanup tools: broom, whisk, and dustpan

A Wonderful Indoor Window Box

This flower box can add a new feature to the classroom and warmth to the environment.

1. Attach an old window frame, without the glass, to a wall.
2. Under the frame, secure brackets to the wall.
3. Rest the flower box (redwood or plastic) on the brackets.
4. Line the flower box with plastic.
5. Line the bottom with pebbles or stones.
6. Fill with potting soil and shade-loving plants.

Good Bulb Possibilities

Another group of plants that can add blooms and color to the class-room are bulbs.

Crocus. If you plant these in the fall, they will be the first sign of spring when they bloom outdoors. They grow low and close to the soil. They come in a variety of colors to provide a contrasting display.

Daffodil. These can be planted outside in the fall, and they will bloom in the spring. You can also force them to bloom in the classroom.

Hyacinth. These bulbs produce a long bloom on the end of their stem. They can be grown outside or within the classroom space. Their sweet aroma provides another sensory experience for children to enjoy.

Narcissus and Amaryllis. Purchase Narcissus bulbs (also called paper-whites) at garden centers. Choose healthy bulbs with no deep scars. Plant 5 to 6 bulbs in each container to produce an effective show of

blooms. There are several different ways to plant the paper-whites.
1) Grow them in water, but make sure the water only touches the roots.
2) Plant them in gravel in shallow pots. Again, make sure the water only touches the roots and not the bulb. 3) Plant them in regular potting soil. Fill a large pot with 2" (5 cm) of soil, add the bulbs with the points up, and add more potting soil. (Be careful not to cover the points of bulbs with soil.) Within 3 to 4 weeks, you will have blooming paper-whites that are a beautiful addition to the environment. They also add a wonderful smell for all to enjoy.

Like the Narcissus, you can also force Amaryllis to bloom during the winter. They come in many colorful varieties that provide a welcome spark to the classroom space.

Garden Plants That Come Inside

You can move some garden plants indoors for all to enjoy. These include fuchsia, geranium, hibiscus, impatiens, petunia, rose, gloxinia, and snapdragon.

Avoid These Plants

Some plants should **not** be in an environment with children. Just like all the other classroom materials, plants must be non-toxic because young children will taste and mouth most items in their environment. The following plants can cause allergic reactions, skin irritations, or internal poisoning. These should **never** be in an early childhood classroom.

  Aloe (aloe barbadensis)
  Asparagus Fern (asparagus plumasus)
  Caladium (caladium xanthosoma)
  Castorbean (ricinum communis)
  Dumbcane (dieffenbachia)
  Elephant's Ear (colocasia esculentum)
  English Ivy (hedera helix)
  Holly Berries
  Lantana (lantana amara)
  Mistletoe (loranthaeceae)
  Philodendron (golden pothos)
  Poinsettia (euphorbia pulcherrima)

A Place to Begin: Growing Plants

Check your classroom to determine a good place to grow plants. Armed with the list of hardy plants included in this chapter, go to a greenhouse or home store. Select a large plant and several small plants that you can grow together in your classroom. Remember, most plants grow better when grouped because they create their own environmental system. Place these plants in a large pot with a hole in the bottom and a saucer to catch the run-off. Then, put them in an area of the classroom that gets some sun and can be reached by children. To protect the floor surface from possible water leaks, place a sheet of plastic or a large tray under the plants. Mark a clear plastic measuring cup with the amount of water needed by the plants in the space. This will help children take care of the watering on a weekly basis. (Keep in mind that more plants die from over-watering than from a lack of water.) After you add the plants to the classroom, observe their positive effect on the environment.

chapter 10
Extending Your Understanding

To further expand your understanding of early childhood environments, read and reflect on some of the classics in the field. These helpful resources will build on the contents of this book and provide insight into the Reggio Emilia program and other innovative places for young children, their teachers, and parents.

Cadwell, L. B. (1997). *Bringing Reggio Emilia home: An innovative approach to early childhood education*. New York: Teachers College Press.

This book records Cadwell's year of learning in a Reggio Emilia school. It includes her experiences with applying these principles in The College School, St. Louis, Missouri.

City of Reggio Emilia. (1996). *The hundred languages of children (Catalogue of the exhibit)*. Distributed in the U.S. by Reggio Children USA.

This beautifully illustrated book describes the elements of The Hundred Languages exhibit that has toured around the world. Text is in Italian and English, with photographs of the schools and children's artwork from the Reggio Schools.

Edwards, C. P., L. Gandini, & G. E. Forman, (Eds.). (1993). *The hundred languages of children: The Reggio Emilia approach to early childhood education* (1st ed.). Norwood, NJ: Ablex Publishing Corporation.
This is the first introduction to the Reggio Emilia program in Italy. It is the place to begin reading about this very special environment.

Edwards, C. P., L. Gandini, & G. E. Forman, (Eds.). (1998). *The hundred languages of children: The Reggio Emilia approach–Advanced reflections* (2nd ed.). Norwood, NJ: Ablex Publishing Corporation.
This is a second view of the Reggio Emilia program. It provides the principles of the approach and application of the program.

Gandini, L. (1993). Fundamentals of the Reggio Emilia approach to early childhood. *Young Children,* 49 (1), 4-8.
This is a short article that provides basic information about the Reggio approach.

Greenman, J. (1988). *Caring spaces, learning places: Children's environments that work*. Redmond, WA: Exchange Press, Inc.
This is a classic text that can assist in understanding the needs of young children in a childcare environment.

Greenman, J. *Great places for childhood: Creating children's environments that work*. Kaplan: Lewisville, NC.
This video uses a variety of appropriate environments to illustrate that children need places to be messy, active, creative, and quiet. A facilitator's guide provides additional information about making spaces work for children and teachers.

Greenman, J. & A. Stonehouse. (1998). *Places for childhoods: Making quality happen in the real world*. Redmond, WA: Exchange Press, Inc.
This very insightful book deals with issues that relate to quality childcare. It includes reflections by early childhood experts on the realities of today's world of childcare.

Hendricks, J. (Ed.). (1996). *First steps toward teaching the Reggio way*. Saddle River, NJ: Prentice Hall.
This is an excellent introduction to the Reggio Emilia schools. It includes several sections that describe American interpretations of the Reggio approach.

Innovations in early childhood education. In P. Weissman (Ed.), *The international Reggio newsletter*. The Merrill-Palmer Institute, 71-A East Ferry Avenue, Detroit, MI 48202.
This newsletter focuses on the Reggio Emilia approach and programs that are attempting to implement the principles.

Katz, L. & S. C. Chard. (1997). *Engaging children's minds: The project approach*. Norwood, NJ: Ablex Publishing Corporation.
This is a comprehensive discussion of the project approach. It includes information about planning and implementing projects in early childhood programs.

Topal, C. W. & L. Gandini. (1999). *Beautiful stuff!: Learning with found materials*. Worchester, MA: Davis Publications, Inc.
This very visual book describes a project that is built on the collection of beautiful materials. Photographs and text demonstrate how young children make discoveries and connections with the unique natural materials.

References

The Australian Woman's Weekly Craft Library. (1997). *Soft furnishings & designer trims.* Sydney, Australia: ACP Publishing.

Barclay, K., C. Benelli, & A. Curtis. (1995). Literacy begins at birth: What caregivers can learn from parents of children who read early. *Young Children,* 50 (4), 20-28.

Barker, L. (1995). *The creative nursery.* London, England: Salamander Books.

Better Homes and Gardens (Ed.). (1983). *Stretching living space.* Des Moines, IA: Better Homes and Gardens Books.

Better Homes and Gardens Decorating (Ed.). (Spring, 1991). Blueprints to grow by. *Bedroom and Bath Ideas,* 60-65. Des Moines, IA: Better Homes and Gardens Decorating Ideas.

Better Homes and Gardens Decorating (Ed.). (Spring, 1991). The Butlers did it. *Bedroom and Bath Ideas,* 55-59. Des Moines, IA: Better Homes and Gardens Decorating Ideas.

Better Homes and Gardens Decorating (Ed.). (1981). *Window Shelves. Window and Wall Decorating Ideas*, 74-81. Des Moines, IA: Better Homes and Gardens Decorating Ideas.

Blaska, J. K. & R. Hasslen. (1994). Environmental impact: What we can learn from Swedish early childhood settings. *Day Care and Early Education*, 22, 29-33.

Brann, D. R. (1978). *How to construct built-in and sectional book-cases*. Briarcliffe Manor, NY: Easi-Bild Directions Simplified, Inc.

Bredekamp, S. & C. Copple. (1997). *Developmentally appropriate practice in early childhood programs*. Washington, DC: National Association for the Education of Young Children (NAEYC).

Cadwell, L. B. (1997). *Bringing Reggio Emilia home: An innovative approach to early childhood education*. New York: Teachers College Press.

Ceppi, G. & M. Zini. (1998). *Children, spaces, relations: Metaproject for an environment for young children*. Reggio Emilia, Italy: Reggio Children.

Church, E. B. (1996). Your learning environment. *Scholastic Early Childhood Today*, 10 (8), 31-33.

Conran, T. (1992). *Toys and children's furniture*. London, England: Conran Octopus.

Department of the Army. (Effective 12 March 1990). Regulation 608-10. *Personal affairs: Child development services*. Unclassified. 166.

DeStefano, K. (1999). Weekend decorating projects. *All Wound Up*, 9 (1).

Edwards, C. P., L. Gandini, & G. E. Forman (Eds.). (1993). *The hundred languages of children: The Reggio Emilia approach to early childhood education* (1st ed.). Norwood, NJ: Ablex Publishing Corporation.

Edwards, C. P., L. Gandini, & G. E. Forman (Eds.). (1998). *The hundred languages of children: The Reggio Emilia approach–Advanced reflections* (2nd ed.). Norwood, NJ: Ablex Publishing Corporation.

Essa, E. & R. Young. (1994). *Introduction to early childhood education*. Toronto, Canada: Nelson Canada.

Ewing, J. & E. A. Eddowes. (1994). Sand play in the primary classroom. *Dimensions of Early Childhood*, 22 (4), 24-25.

Feeney, S. & E. Moravick. (1987). A thing of beauty: Aesthetic development in young children. *Young Children*, 42 (6), 7-15.

Feldman, J. R. (1997). *Wonderful rooms where children can bloom! Over 500 innovative ideas and activities for your child-centered classroom*. Peterborough, NH: Crystal Springs Books.

Firlik, R. (1994). Promoting development through constructing appropriate environments: Preschools in Reggio Emilia, Italy. *Day Care and Early Education, 22* (1), 12-20.

Foa, I. & G. Brin. (1979). *Kids' stuff.* New York, NY: Pantheon Books.

Fraser, S. (2000). *Authentic childhood: Experiencing Reggio Emilia in the classroom.* Scarborough, Ontario, Canada: Nelson Thomson Learning.

Frost, J. L. (1992). Reflections on research and practice in outdoor play environments. *Dimensions of Early Childhood, 20* (4), 10.

Gandini, L. (1994). Special places for children—The schools in Reggio Emilia, Italy. *Child Care Information Exchange, 96,* 47-70.

Gilliatt, M. (1987). *The decorating book.* New York, NY: Pantheon Books.

Gilliatt, M. (1999). *Mary Gilliatt's new guide to decorating.* London, England: Conrad Octopus.

Gilliatt, M. (1984). *Designing rooms for children.* London, England: Little, Brown and Company.

Goldstein, D. (1991). *Physical environment: Planning a supportive environment.* Frankfort, KY: Kentucky State Department of Education. (ERIC Document Reproduction Service No. ED 379 102)

Greenman, J. (1988). *Caring spaces, learning places: Children's environments that work.* Redmond, WA: Exchange Press, Inc.

Greenman, J. (1991). Living in the real world. Babies get out: Outdoor settings for infant toddler play. *Child Care Information Exchange, 79,* 21-24.

Greenman, J. (1998). *Places for childhoods: Making quality happen in the real world.* Redmond, WA: Exchange Press, Inc.

Hannah, G. (1984). Jazzing up your classroom. *Learning, 13* (1), 68-71.

Harms, T. & R. M. Clifford. (1980). *Early childhood environment rating scale.* New York, NY: Teachers College, Columbia University.

Harms, T., D. Cryer, & R. M. Clifford. (1990). *Infant/toddler environment rating scale.* New York, NY: Teachers College, Columbia University.

Health and Welfare Canada. (1993). *Facilities & equipment for day care centres.* Ottawa, Canada: Health and Welfare Canada.

Hildebrand, V. (1987). Organizing: A key aspect of classroom management. *Dimensions of Early Childhood, 15,* 14-16.

Hiss, T. (1990). *The experience of place: A new way of looking at and dealing with our radically changing cities and countryside.* New York, NY: Vintage Books.

Jones, E. & E. Prescott. (1978). *Dimensions of teaching–learning environments. II. Focus on day care*. Pasadena, CA. (ERIC Document Reproduction Service No. ED 108 579)

Katz, L. & S. C. Chard. (1997). *Engaging children's minds: The project approach*. Norwood, NJ: Ablex Publishing Corporation.

Keevill, E. (1995). *Decorating your child's room*. London, England: Ward Lock.

Kritchevsky, S., E. Prescott, & L. Walling. (1977). *Planning environments for young children's physical space* (2nd ed.). Washington, DC: National Association for the Education of Young Children (NAEYC).

Lang, S. (1993). *Ideas for great kids' rooms*. Menlo Park, CA: Sunset Books, Inc.

Logrippo, R. (1995). *In my world: Designing living and learning environments for the young*. New York, NY: John Wiley & Sons, Inc.

Lott, J. (1989). *Children's rooms*. New York, NY: Prentice Hall.

Loughlin, C. E. & J. H. Suina. (1982). *The learning environment: An instructional strategy*. New York, NY: Teachers College, Columbia University.

MacDonald, M. (1989). Deinstitutionalizing architecture for children: The Stanford arboretum children's center. *Children's Environment Quarterly*, 6 (4), 40-47.

Malaguzzi, L. (1994). Your image of the child: Where teaching begins. (B. Rankin, L. Morrow, & L. Gandini, Trans.) In L. Gandini (Ed.), *Child Care Information Exchange: "Special places for children–The schools in Reggio Emilia, Italy"* (96, 47-70). Redmond, WA: Child Care Information Exchange (Original work from a seminar presented June 1993).

Manroe, C. O. (1997). *Uncluttered: Storage room by room*. London, England: Aurum Press.

McGuire, K. (1994). *Building outdoor play structures*. New York, NY: Sterling Publishing Company, Inc.

Miller, K. (1987). Room arrangement: Making it work for you & your kids. *Scholastic Pre-K Today*, 2 (1), 27-32.

Moore, G. T. (1994). *Early childhood physical environment observation schedules and rating scales: Preliminary scales for the measurement of the physical environments*. (Report No. ISBN-0-938 744-83-6: R94-2). Milwaukee, WI: University of Wisconsin, School of Architecture. (ERIC Document Reproduction Service No. ED 377 950)

Myers, B. K. & K. Maurer. (1987). Teaching with less talking: Learning centers in the kindergarten. *Young Children*, 42 (5), 20-27.

National Association for the Education of Young Children. (1998). *Accreditation criteria & procedures of the national association for the education of young children*. Washington, DC: National Association for the Education of Young Children (NAEYC).

National Association for the Education of Young Children. (1998). *Guide to accreditation by the national association for the education of young children: Self-study, validation, and accreditation*. Washington, DC: National Association for the Education of Young Children (NAEYC)

Novelli, J. (1991). Instruction style meets classroom design. *Instructor*, 100 (1), 26-30.

Olds, A. R. (1979). Designing developmentally optimal classrooms for children with special needs. In Samuel J. Meisels (Ed.), *Special education and development: Perspectives on young children with special needs* (91-138). Baltimore, MD: University Park Press.

Olds, A. R. (1982). Planning a developmentally optimal day care center. *Day Care Journal*. Washington, DC: Day Care Council of America.

Olds, A. R. (1987). Designing settings for infants and toddlers. In C. S. Weinstein & T. G. David (Eds.), *Spaces for children: The built environment and child development* (117-138). New York, NY: Plenum Press.

Owen, C. & P. Gorton. (1998). *Storage solutions*. London: Quadrillion Publishing.

Prescott, E. & T. G. David. (1976). *Concept paper on the effects of the physical environment on day care*. Washington, DC: Department of Health, Education, and Welfare. (ERIC Document Reproduction Service No. ED 156 356)

Prescott, E. (1974). Approaches to quality in early childhood programs. *Childhood Education*, 50 (3), 125-131.

Prescott, E., S. Kritchevsky, & E. Jones. (1972). *The day care environmental checklist. Assessment of child-rearing environments: An ecological approach* (Part 1 of final report). Pasadena, CA: Pacific Oaks College. (ERIC Document Reproduction Service No. ED 076 228)

Prescott, E., S. Kritchevsky, & E. Jones. (1973). *Who thrives in group day care? Assessment of child-rearing environments: An ecological approach* (Part 2 of final report). Pasadena, CA: Pacific Oaks College. (ERIC Document Reproduction Service No. ED 076 229)

Sanoff, H. & J. Sanoff. (1988). *Learning environments for children* (2nd ed.). Atlanta, GA: Humanics Limited.

Sanoff, H. (1995). *Creating environments for young children*. Raleigh, NC: North Carolina State University, School of Design. (ERIC Document Reproduction Service No. ED 394 640)

Shoulberg, W. (1989). Baby rooms: *Creating the perfect space for your baby to grow in*. Los Angeles, CA: HP Books.

Sloane, M. W. (2000). Make the most of learning centers. *Dimensions in Early Childhood*, 28 (1), 16-20.

Taylor, A. (1993). How schools are redesigning their space. *Educational Leadership*, 51 (1), 36-41.

Topal, C. W. & L. Gandini. (1999). *Beautiful stuff!: Learning with found materials*. Worcester, MA: Davis Publications, Inc.

Torelli, L. & C. Durrett. (1998). *Landscapes for learning: Designing group care environments for infants, toddlers and two-year-olds*. Berkeley, CA: Torelli/Durrett Infant & Toddler Childcare Furniture.

Torrice, A. F. & R. Logrippo. (1989). *In my room: Designing for and with children*. New York, NY: Fawcett Columbine.

Trawick-Smith, J. (1992). Review of research: The classroom environment affects children's play and development. *Dimensions, 20* (2), 27-30.

Vergeront, J. (1987). *Places and spaces for preschool and primary (indoors)*. Washington, DC: National Association for the Education of Young Children (NAEYC).

Vergeront, J. (1988). *Places and spaces for preschool and primary (outdoors)*. Washington, DC: National Association for the Education of Young Children (NAEYC).

Whitehead, L. C. & S. I. Ginsberg. (1999). Creating a family-like atmosphere in child care settings: All the more difficult in large child care centers. *Young Children, 54* (2), 4-10.

Woman's Day. (1987). A room of my own. *Home Decorating Ideas*, (June), 74-83.

Appendices A

Appendix A

INVENTORY FORM

Inventory					Date
Item	**Location**	**Source**	**Purchase Date**	**Cost**	**Insured Value**

Appendix B

EQUIPMENT CHECKLIST

Basic Items

_____ unlined paper

_____ colored paper

_____ pencils

_____ markers

_____ children's books (10-15)

_____ computer

_____ electrical outlet strip

_____ strip light

_____ low table and chairs

_____ area rug

_____ scissors

_____ paper punch

_____ clear tape

_____ masking tape

_____ display board

_____ folders

_____ trash can

Optional Items

_____ typewriter and typing paper

_____ computer printer

_____ decorative materials: ribbon, yarn, glitter, stickers, buttons, and so on

_____ soft pillows

_____ rulers

Items to Be Collected

_____ cardboard pieces

APPENDIX C

ENVIRONMENT SCAN

Classroom Area Date

1.   What do you see?

2.   How do you feel about what you see?

3.   What do you like?

4.   What don't you like?

5.   How does this compare to any of your other experiences?

6.   What environmental principles are being applied?

7.   What have you discovered?

Appendix D

TEAM INVENTORY

The following information can be helpful to the successful completion
of a project or design.

Check those special abilities that apply to you.

I can

_____ hammer nails into lumber to create a useful unit.

_____ insert hanging hardware into the walls.

_____ operate an electric drill or electric screwdriver.

_____ operate an electric handsaw.

_____ make wooden items that require cutting lumber.

_____ assemble items.

_____ paint with a brush.

_____ paint with a roller.

_____ use stencils for decoration.

_____ apply other decorative painting techniques,

such as _____ .

_____ apply wallpaper and/or border.

_____ lay carpet or other flooring.

_____ apply decorative techniques to furniture, floors, or walls.

_____ sew with a machine.

_____ sew by hand.

_____ knit or crochet.

_____ weave.

_____ illustrate.

_____ organize materials.

_____ grow plants.

_____ solicit donations.

Areas of greatest interest _____

_____

Areas of least interest _____

_____

I can help others learn to _____

_____

Name _____ Date _____

APPENDIX E

SPACE—MATERIALS/EQUIPMENT—ACTIVITIES PROFILE

Room or Area: _____ Date: _____

Window Placement: _____

Lighting Sources: _____

Range of Activities:

Specialized Use:

Materials/Equipment Listing

Item	Condition Poor—Good—Excellent	Current Use Well—Limited—Poor
1.		
2.		
3.		
4.		
5.		
6.		
7.		
8.		
9.		
10.		
11.		
12.		

Recommendations:

APPENDIX F

WALL FASTENERS, SUPPORT SYSTEMS, AND SPAN DISTANCES

Types of Wall Fasteners

1. General-purpose, plain plastic anchor for use in brick and high-density blocks and concrete
2. Heavy-duty, plastic anchor with ribbed lower end to prevent pulling out of loose material
3. Finned, concrete block anchor (can be hammered in) for concrete or concrete block walls
4. Gypsum board plugs (collapsible or barbed)
5. Spring toggles for lath and plaster

Shelving Support Systems

Name	Type	Use
Wooden Batten	fixed	alcove and closets
Cantilever	fixed	light loads in any position
Steel Angle	fixed	any position
Gallows Bracket	fixed	any position
Metal Uprights (back)	adjustable	movable metal brackets in any position
Metal Uprights (sides)	adjustable	movable support clips in any position
Groove Shelves	adjustable	alcove and light loads

Support Span Distances

Material	Thickness	Span
Acrylic	½"	22"
Board lumber (12" wide)	1"	24"
Board lumber (12" wide)	2"	56"
Glass	⅜"	18"
Melamine	¾"	36"
Particle (chip) board	¾"	28"
Plywood	¾"	36"

APPENDIX G

Funnel Holder

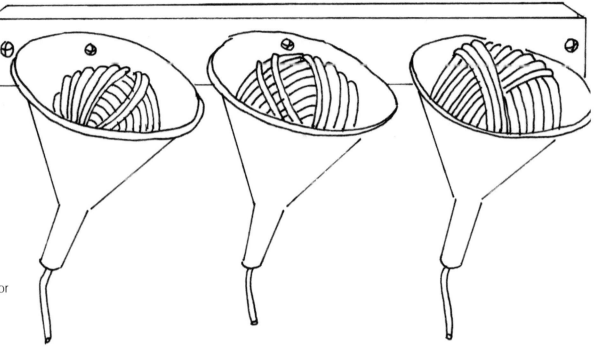

Materials
Strip of wood
Large-headed screws
Screwdriver
Paint and brush
Drill
Metal or plastic funnels, varied or uniform sizes
Washers, if needed

How to Make
1. Mount a strip of wood, 1" x 2" (2 cm x 5 cm) or larger, on the wall. (The size of the wood depends on the number of funnels you are going to attach.)
2. Paint the board to match the wall.
3. Pre-drill a single hole 1" (2 cm) below the rim of the funnel. This step is essential if you are using plastic funnels—it will ensure a longer life for plastic products.
4. Attach the funnels to the board with large-headed screws. Add washers if the funnels move about when used. The washer will prevent the screw from working its way through the funnel's surface.

How to Use
- Funnels are useful for dispensing thin cord, cotton yarn, string, or wool. It is best to place the funnels where these items will be used.
- Tie scissors to a string and hang nearby for snipping off exact lengths.

Drawstring Bag

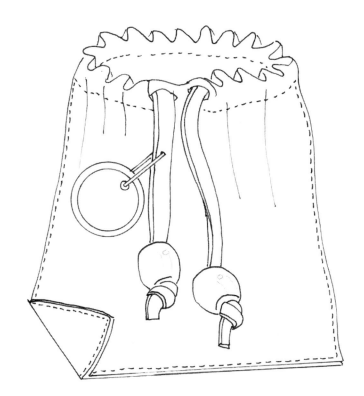

Materials
Fabric in a sturdy weave
Scissors
Straight pins
Needle and thread
Iron
Rope or ribbon drawstring (twice the size of the bag opening)
Two wooden beads
Metal-rimmed tag
Length of yarn

How to Make
1. Cut two rectangular pieces of fabric the appropriate size for the item to be stored.
2. Pin together the wrong sides of the fabric.
3. Stitch together the sides and bottom edges. Double stitch all seams to ensure durability.
4. Turn the bag right side out.
5. Fold over the opening edge about 1 ½" (4 cm) and turn under the raw edge about ⅜" (9 mm).
6. Press the seam edges with a hot iron; pin them in position.
7. Mark the location for a pair of cord openings on the upper edge seam.
8. Make two small buttonholes ⅝" (15 mm) below the upper edge.
9. Pin the upper seam (cord channel) in place and stitch the cord channel seam in place.
10. Thread the cord through the channel.
11. Make a single tight knot, several inches from both ends of the cord. Thread one bead onto each cord. Knot again to keep each bead in place.
12. Attach a metal-rimmed tag to the drawstring with yarn.

How to Use
- Bags of various sizes are suitable for storing objects that are medium- to lightweight.
- Toys that have many small parts or items that are best kept together are well suited for this form of storage.
- Place the bags on open shelves or suspend them from wall hooks.
- Label the metal-rimmed tag, clearly and boldly, on both sides for easy identification.
- Laminated homemade tags are just as durable and less expensive than the metal-rimmed tags.

Cylinder Container

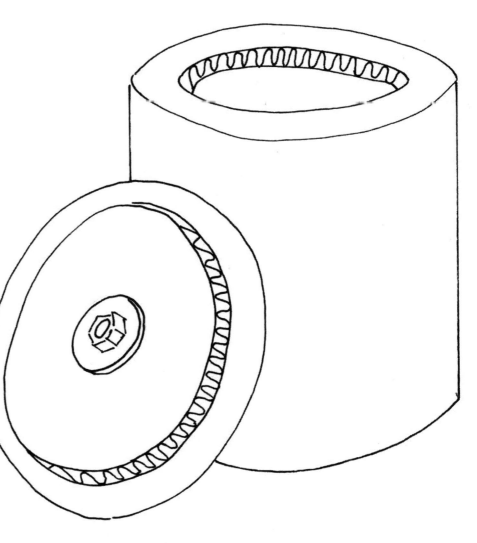

Materials
Heavy paper tubes in a variety of sizes (the type used in cement works)
Saw (electric or handsaw)
Cardboard
Pen
Scissors
Glue
Weight
Drill
Wooden bead
Bolt, ring washer, and nut
Paint or markers

How to Make
1. Use an electric or handsaw to cut the tube the desired size.
2. Trace the circumference of the tube onto a sheet of two-ply cardboard. Cut out two circles, one to use for the bottom of the cylinder and the other for the fitted cover.
3. Glue one of the large circles to the base of the cylinder unit. Place a weight on top until it is dry.
4. Measure the inner circumference of the tube. Cut out a cardboard circle slightly smaller than this measurement. This piece will become part of the cover.
5. Glue together the two cover pieces. Place a weight on top until it is dry.
6. Drill a hole through the center of the cover.
7. Secure a wooden bead to the cover using a bolt, washer, and nut.
8. Paint the cylinder storage unit or color it with markers.

How to Use
- A series of graduated (in size) cylinder storage units have an interesting decorative appeal when placed in a location that cannot accept anything else because of space limitations.
- Cover the units or keep them uncovered. Using various sizes and combinations offer an interesting visual option.
- The cylinders are an interesting addition to the Dramatic Play Area. Use them as props and storage places.
- Cylinders are an inexpensive storage option for use in the storage room.

Clothespin Hanger

Material
Wooden, spring-loaded clothespins
Drill
Screws
Screwdriver
Wooden board
Paint and brushes, optional

How to Make

1. Pre-drill the clothespins and secure them with screws to the wooden board.
2. Attach the board to the wall using a sufficient number of screws to ensure stable attachment.
3. If desired, paint the pegs and mounting board.

How to Use

- Place small wooden strips with clothespins around the classroom to hang children's notes and drawings.
- If you place the clothespin unit at the classroom's hall entrance, those who pass by will notice the pictures and messages.
- In storage areas, a clothespin unit can help with inventory control or to note the arrival of new materials.

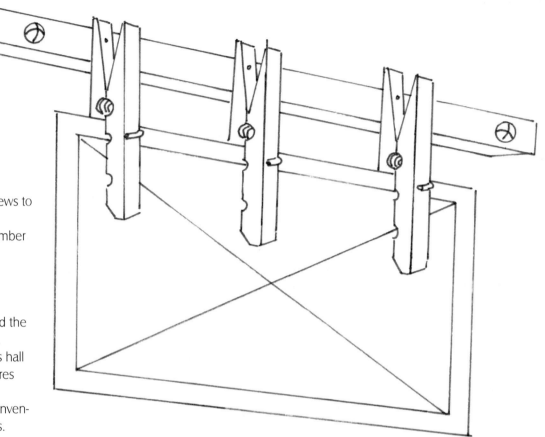

Wire Hanger

Materials
Ruler
Sturdy wire hanger
Closely woven fabric
Scissors
Bias tape trim
Needle and thread
Press-and-close closure tape

How to Make
1. Using a ruler, measure the cross bar of the wire hanger.
2. Cut fabric to match the width of the cross bar. This will be the background for the hanging device.
3. Cut a second piece of fabric to be the pockets. Cut this piece as wide as the entire hanger. The extra size will make it easier to put items in and out of the pockets.
4. Bind the raw edges of the pocket fabric. The sizes of the pockets and their position on the background fabric can vary.
5. Pin and sew the pockets in position. Sew bias tape trim to the background fabric's raw edges.
6. Stitch press-and-close closure tape to the top of the wire hanger.
7. Attach the hanging device to the cross bar of the hanger.

How to Use
- The Wire Hanger offers endless possibilities for storing and organizing items such as paper and pens.
- Use this storage idea in the Art Area to keep rulers, markers, and other tools within easy reach.
- In the classroom storage area, use the Wire Hanger to store yardsticks and paintbrushes.

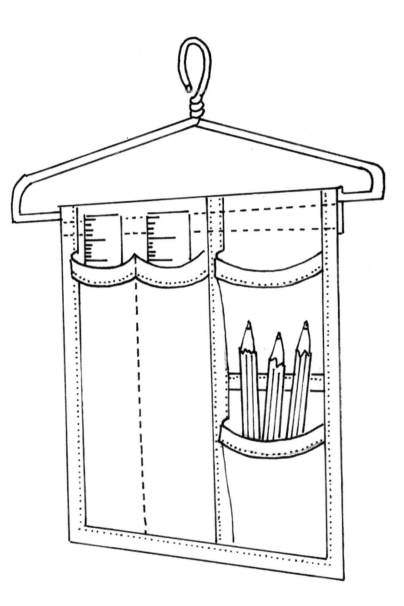

Berry Pail

Materials
Plastic berry pail or a metal pail (both with a secure handle)
Tape measure
Fabric in a sturdy weave
Scissors
Bias tape trim
Needle and thread
Straight pins

How to Make
1. Clean and sanitize the pail.
2. Measure the circumference of the pail and cut a length of fabric to match.
3. Cut a second length of fabric half the size of the pail's depth.
4. Sew bias tape trim along the two edges of the large and small lengths of fabric.
5. Attach ties to the edges of both lengths of fabric.
6. Sew bias tape trim along the two raw edges of the narrow pocket fabric.
7. Determine the number of pockets you want and their size.
8. Pin the pocket strip in place.
9. Stitch the lower edge of the pocket-making strip to the larger pail-covering fabric.
10. Mark the locations of the pocket-creating seams. Sew to create individual pockets.

How to Use
- The pail and cover offer storage both inside and outdoors.
- The pail is useful for keeping assorted play materials together. (For example, fill the pail with small blocks and put vehicles and miniature people in the pockets.)
- In the Book Area, use the pail to hold a storybook and larger props and the pockets to store the smaller accessories.
- In the Block Area, store colorful lengths of wood in the pail. In the pockets, store recycled items that offer new options for block play.

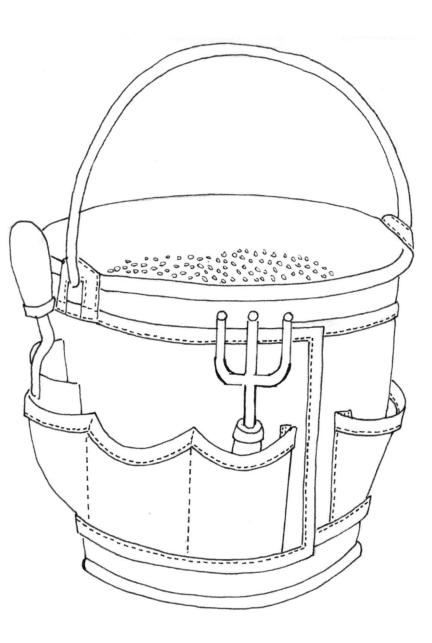

Clay Tiles

Materials

Clay tiles in assorted sizes and shapes (square, round, rectangular)
Water and brush, if needed
Sandpaper, if needed

How to Make

1. If using new tiles, simply select a site within the classroom and stack them. Make sure that the stacked tiles are well balanced and present no danger of slipping.
2. If using older tiles, keep in mind that they often have character and color variations. Use clear water and a brush to try and restore them to a respectable state. If you are unsuccessful, do not use them.
3. Be wary of any chipped surfaces that are unsafe or burrs of clay on the inside of flues. Sand these burrs to produce a smooth surface.

How to Use

- Arrange collected tiles according to what they will hold.
- Identify the type of storage you need and use the tiles as needed. For example, stand tiles on end to hold lengths of fabric in the Dramatic Play Center or lengths of wood in the Block Area.
- Place tiles in a resting arrangement to make miniature shelves for small blocks and vehicles.

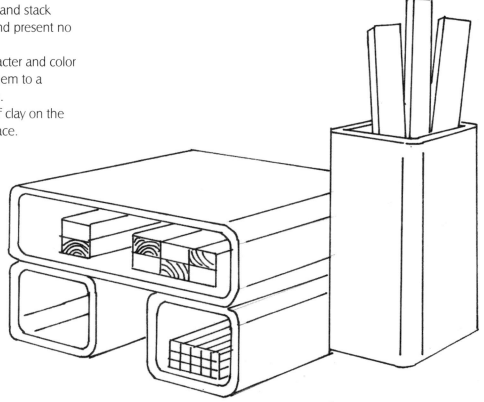

Juice Jugs

Materials

Clear juice jugs, assorted sizes and shapes
Pen
Craft knife
Medium- and fine-grade sandpaper

How to Make

1. Rinse and sanitize the juice jugs. Remove the labels by soaking them in water. Some glues are difficult to remove—in some cases, liquid floor wax works well.
2. Determine what portion of the jug you are going to remove. Mark it lightly with a pen.
3. Turn the jug on its side and insert the knife blade into the plastic surface above the pen line. Cut slowly and steadily toward the pen marking. Maintain a firm and even cutting stroke to attain a smooth edge.
4. Remove the top of the jug and think about where and how you can use it.
5. First, use medium-grade sandpaper on the rim. Remove all the plastic burrs created during the cutting process. Next, use a finer grade of sandpaper. Continue sanding until the jug rim is smooth. Stop sanding when you attain the smoothest and safest surface.

How to Use

- Clear jugs offer a transparent view of their contents. Therefore, you can use these containers throughout the classroom for many purposes.
- Use the containers to hold creative materials that are ready for use or to store materials until they are needed.
- These containers offer an easy way to sort crayons by color. Displaying the crayons in this manner highlights the colors.
- Small items, such as beads, become more interesting to the eye when stored in these clear containers.
- Small, clear containers make excellent paint pots.

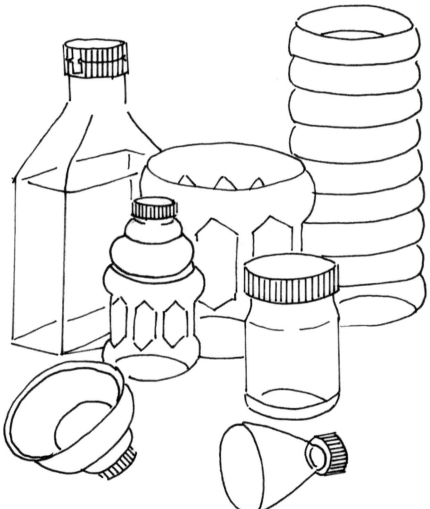

Fabric Container Holder

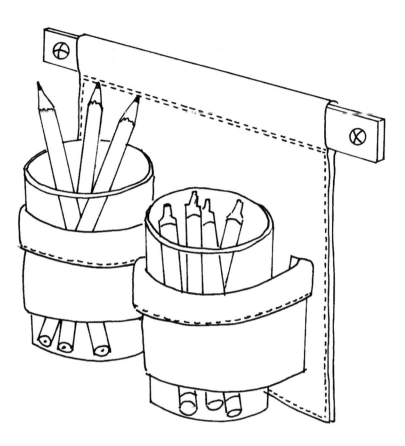

Materials

Preshrunk fabric in a sturdy weave
Scissors
Strip of wood, 1" x 12" (2 cm x 30 cm) long
Tape measure
Two clear plastic containers
Elastic
Needle and thread
Screws

How to Make

1. Cut out a square of sturdy fabric or create a sturdy square by sewing together two layers of thinner fabric. (This will be the backing.)
2. Create a channel that is slightly larger than the strip of wood.
3. Measure the circumference of the plastic containers. This measurement is the approximate length of fabric you will need to make the two elastic/fabric units to hold the containers.
4. Cut doubles of fabric to make the container holder strips.
5. Fold down the upper edge. Stitch the fold in place. Make it large enough to slip the elastic through easily. Do not put elastic in at this time, though.
6. Cut the fabric length into two equal pieces.
7. Thread the elastic pieces into position through each portion.
8. Position the holder units on the square fabric backing; stitch in place.
9. Slide the wooden strip through the fabric backing's channel.
10. Screw the wooden strip into position on the wall.

How to Use

- This holder is ideal for the Creative Area. It is great for holding crayons or pens.
- It is especially practical to keep the holder next to the chalkboard. If the containers are large enough, store chalk in one unit and erasers in the other.
- Another practical location for the holder is at the magnet board to hold all the magnets.
- If the holder becomes soiled, remove and launder it.

Two Tier Cardboard Shelf

Materials
Three-ply cardboard
Hand or electric saw
Ruler

How to Make

1. Cut a piece of three-ply cardboard 48" (120 cm) long and 24" (60 cm) wide.
2. Measure and crease the cardboard 9" (22 cm) in from each end, making two wing sides. The cardboard should now stand upright.
3. Cut two slots into the 24" x 9" (60 cm x 22 cm) wings.
4. Cut two lengths of cardboard 9" x 30" (22 cm x 75 cm).
5. Position the two shelf pieces into the two pairs of slots.

How to Use

- This small shelf unit provides space for storing paper and other creative tools and materials used in the Creative Center.
- Shelving units can vary in size and configuration to meet storage needs. Simply change the height, width, and size of the shelving compartment and functional storage space multiplies.
- Make larger units to use in the storage room.

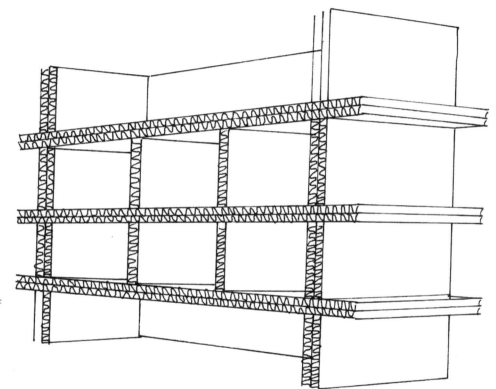

Picture Display and Storage

Materials

Thick, clear plastic
Scissors
Bias tape trim
Needle and thread
Sturdy fabric, 30" x 36" (75 cm x 90 cm)
Two 36" (90 cm) pieces of wood
Screws or eyehooks and picture hooks

How to Make

1. Cut out strips of plastic to suit the size of the pictures you will be displaying or storing.
2. Sew bias tape trim to one edge of each strip of plastic.
3. Position the plastic pieces on the fabric backing; sew in place.
4. Create individual pockets by stitching through the plastic surfaces.
5. Sew bias tape trim around the entire piece of the background fabric.
6. Turn down the upper and lower edges of the fabric to form a channel for the two wooden pieces. Sew in place. Insert a piece of wood through each channel.
7. Mount the storage unit to a wall using screws or eyehooks and picture hooks.

How to Use

- Put magazine photos or photographs of children and families into the clear plastic pockets.
- The unit also can hold small display items, such as small puppets, wee books, or special toys.

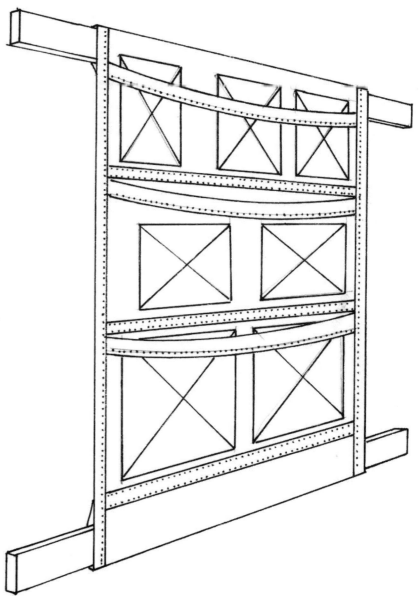

Hanging Rack

Materials

Grosgrain ribbon, 11' (3 m)
Scissors
Straight pins
Pen
Needle and thread
Five wooden slats, 30" (75 cm) long
Four round metal rings
S-hooks

How to Make

1. Cut the ribbon into four equal pieces. Pin together two pieces of ribbon. Do the same with the remaining two pieces.
2. On both sets of ribbons, mark where the wooden slats will be located.
3. Stitch together both sets of ribbons, stitching close to the outer edges. Leave the marked areas open to create channels for the wooden slats.
4. Stitch metal rings at the bottom and top of the two strips of ribbon.
5. Insert the five wooden slats through the channels.
6. Mount the hanging rack to a wall.
7. Place S-hoods strategically on the wooden cross pieces (see illustration).

How to Use

- Use the hanging rack to hold drawstring bags.
- Store items with loops or hanging holes, such as paintbrushes, on the rack.
- Use the rack as a home for puppets or stuffed animals.

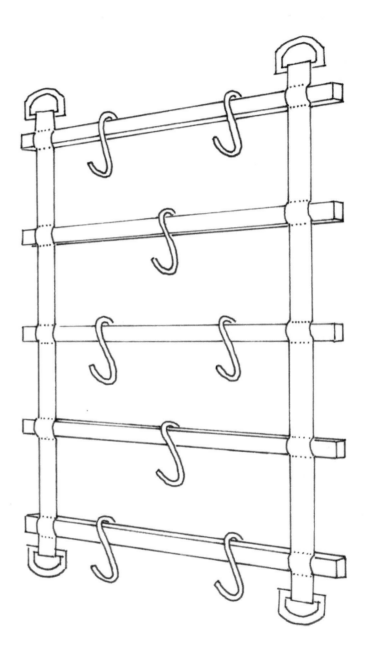

Protected Board

Materials

Piece of plywood, 24" x 36" (60 cm x 90 cm)
Saw
Drill
Thin cork
Glue
Clear plastic, 24" x 30" (60 cm x 75 cm)
Scissors
Small strip of molding, 24" (60 cm) long
Short screws

How to Make

1. Cut plywood to size and create a sculptured upper edge (see illustration).
2. Drill two holes equidistant from each other within the sculptured area.
3. Glue thin cork in place on the lower portion of the plywood.
4. Cut a piece of clear plastic to cover the cork area.
5. Using short shank screws, attach a strip of wooden molding to the plastic to secure it in position.

How to Use

- This is a great way to post delicate or paper items. Just slip them under the clear plastic.
- Place the board where posted items are in danger of getting soiled or wet.
- This board is great to use around infants and toddlers.

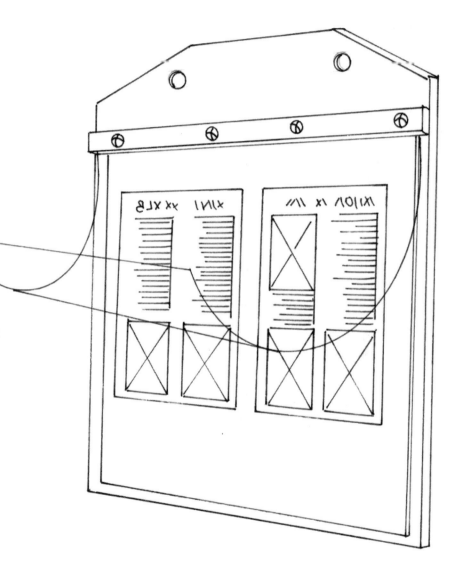

Detachable Pouch

Materials

Fabric with a sturdy weave
Scissors
Marker
Needle and thread
Two brass eyelets
Large, flexible plastic container

How to Make

1. Cut a piece of fabric 3" x 5" (7 cm x 12 cm) to make the back of the pouch.
2. Fold back the fabric ¼" (6 mm), and then ¾" (19 mm) to eliminate the raw edges.
3. Mark two spots equidistant from each other along the upper edge of the fabric (to place the brass eyelets).
4. Cut another piece of fabric 3" x 9" (7 cm x 22 cm) to make the front of the pouch.
5. Fold back the fabric to create a finished seam and a channel.
6. Stitch this piece of fabric to the bottom and the two sides of the back piece.
7. Leave a small opening at the upper side edges to place the plastic stiffening (from the container).
8. Cut out a thin strip (the stiffening) from a plastic container.
9. Insert the plastic strip into the front channel.
10. Attach the brass eyelets.

How to Use

- The brass eyelets offer a location for placing pushpins without destroying the fabric.
- The mouth of the pouch remains open because of the stiffening; therefore, items stored in the pouch are easily accessible at all times.
- Attach a pouch to a bulletin board to hold thumbtacks.
- Use pouches to hold small items used in a classroom setting, such as markers, a small ruler, a small ball of string, and note paper.
- Use a series of larger pouches as a message center for children, teachers, or parents.

Bottle Holder

Materials

Wooden shelf
Saw
Narrow-necked bottles

How to Make

1. Cut elongated slots into the edges of the shelf (see illustration).
2. Place the necks of the bottles into the slots.

How to Use

- Fill the bottles with assorted dry materials such as rice, beans, and so on. (Use a funnel to pour materials into very narrow-necked bottles.)
- Position the bottles on the rack with or without their lids.
- If the bottles are made of tempered glass, they are reasonably safe to use around children and add an aesthetic element to the classroom setting. Plastic bottles work equally well.

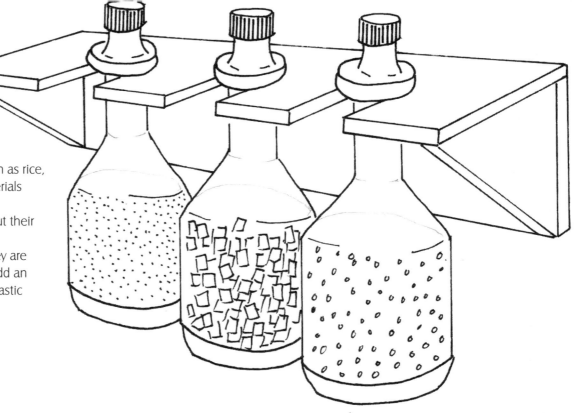

Small Tool Holder

Materials

Quilted fabric
Scissors
Bias tape trim
Needle and thread
Medium-size curtain rings

How to Make

1. Cut a square piece of fabric 12" x 12" (30 cm x 30 cm).
2. Sew bias tape trim along the raw edges of the fabric.
3. When placing the curtain rings, position them equidistant from each other. (Keep in mind the type of items you will store on it.)
4. Cut strips of bias tape for each ring. Sew the strips in place.
5. Cut a longer loop for the ring used to hang the holder.
6. If desired, you can create and suspend larger holders using rings and loops.

How to Use

- Hang a holder near the sink. Store the wooden spoons that the children use to create mixtures in the Creative Center.
- Use smaller and larger rings and store broad- and narrow-handled paint-brushes.
- In the Dramatic Play or Music Center, loop scarves and other delicate fabrics through the rings.

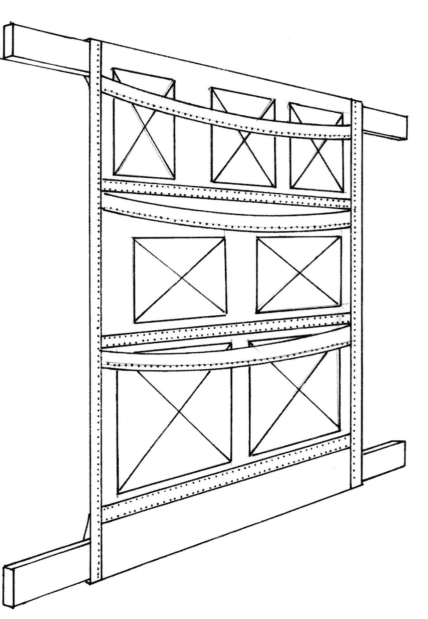

Elasticized Holders

Materials
Double thickness of sturdy fabric
Scissors
Bias tape trim
Needle and thread
Elastic
Dowel, 36″ (1 m) long
Large L-hook

How to Make
1. Cut a length of fabric 34″ (85 cm) long and 24″ (60 cm) wide.
2. Sew bias tape trim around the raw edges of the fabric.
3. Cut a strip of fabric for pockets, 12″ (30 cm) wide and 40″ (100 cm) long.
4. Fold over one of the long edges to create a channel and thread elastic through it.
5. Position the pocket strip and stitch it in place.
6. Create individual pockets by sewing vertically.
7. Adjust the elastic while creating the pocket units.
8. Make three hanging loops and attach them to the upper edge of the fabric.
9. Thread the dowel through the loops. Rest the dowel on a pair of L-hooks.

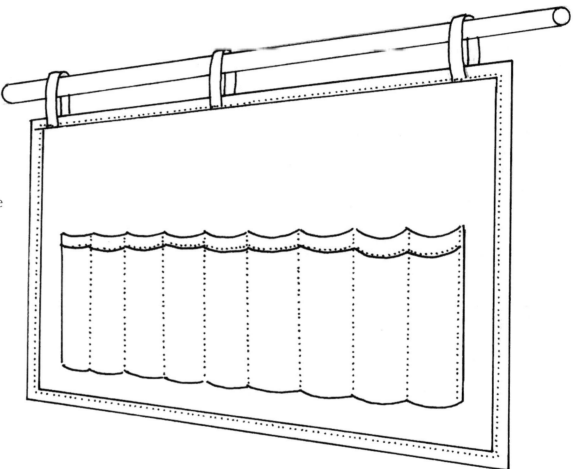

How to Use
- You can place all sorts of items in the pockets. Use the unit either in the classroom or storage area.

Juice Can Storage

Materials

Six large juice cans
Paint and brushes, optional
Wood, 26" x 6" (65 cm x 15 cm)
Saw
Marker
Drill
Two pieces of ¾" (2 cm) dowel
Ribbon, cord, or elastic bands, optional

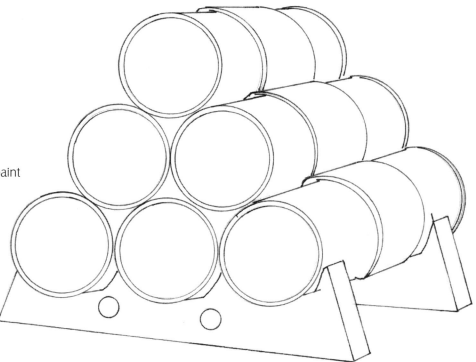

How to Make

1. Clean and sanitize the juice cans. Remove the labels. If desired, paint the cans or do decoupage.
2. Cut two lengths of wood.
3. Taper the ends of each piece of wood to a 45° angle.
4. On one edge of a piece of wood, use a marker to draw the outlines of the circumferences of three cans.
5. Cut out the outlines. Do the same to the remaining piece of wood.
6. Drill two holes equidistant from each other on each end unit.
7. Determine the required length of the dowels by deciding how much of the cans will extend over the resting frame.
8. Place the dowels through the holes of each end unit.
9. If desired, place ribbon, cord, or giant elastic bands around the juice can pyramid before placing the cans on the rack.

How to Use

- This unit is invaluable as the teacher's mail and message center.

Sling Rack

Materials
Wood, 2" x 1" (5 cm x 2 cm)
Saw
Marker
¾" (2 cm) dowels
Glue
Clamps
Fabric with a sturdy weave
Straight pins
Needle and thread

How to Make
1. Cut the wood to make a frame the desired length. Cut the legs and length-wise cross pieces at a 45° angle.
2. Mark where the dowel support pieces will penetrate the four leg units.
3. Draw an outline of where the dowel will rest on the lengths of the wood.
4. Apply glue; wait until tacky. Place the pieces in position and clamp them in place. Allow it to dry.
5. Cut a length of fabric 2 ½ times longer than the rack.
6. Fold and pin the fabric to create channels for the dowel. Sew the channels.
7. Insert the lengths of dowel into each of the sling channels.

How to Use
- Place assorted colored papers on the Sling Rack and put it in the Creative Area. Use a series of these units as mail boxes for children, their art renderings, and take-home messages.
- The size of the sling rack and its dowel size will determine the amount of weight it can hold. The durability of the fabric is also another consideration.
- The depth of the fabric slings will determine how bulky and how big the stored objects can be.
- Use the Sling Rack to store books and magazines or stuffed animals and puppets.
- Since the fabric sling can be removed for washing, use it to collect the children's works and portfolios.
- Place smaller units on tables or on top of toy storage units.
- Use medium-size sling racks in the Dramatic Play Area to store fabric lengths and costume clothing.

Cylinder Shelf

Materials

Three-ply cardboard
Scissors or saw
Marker
Four long, thick cardboard cylinders (medium circumference)
Glue
Weights

How to Make

1. Decide how wide and high you want the shelf unit. Cut the cardboard to suit.
2. Mark where you will put the legs (cardboard cylinders).
3. Glue the legs into position. Apply weights and allow them to dry.
4. Create the desired number of shelf levels. Place one section on top of the other.
5. Identify the spots where one set of legs meets the shelf surface of the other unit. At these spots, glue in place a smaller tube that will fit snuggly into the larger tubes of the legs.

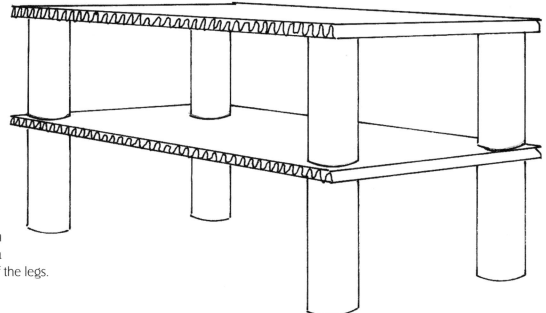

How to Use

- Shelf units can be made in multiples; stack and store as needed.
- The possibility of various sizes adds to their usefulness.
- Children can paint the Cylinder Shelf. If they use tempera paint, cover it with a light coat of varnish to preserve the color pigment and reduce color erosion.

Woven Paper Container

Materials
Old magazines or newspapers
Spray varnish

How to Make
1. Fold magazine or newspaper pages into narrow strips.
2. Begin weaving the strips by creating a cross formation as the base of the container.
3. Add additional strips until the base looks like a star burst.
4. Bend the strips upward.
5. Begin to weave additional strips up the sides of the developing container. Continue adding strips until the sides are complete.
6. Turn back the final inches of paper strips into the container's upper rim.
7. Spray with varnish to give the container some degree of waterproofing and stability.

How to Use
- Several coats of varnish make the container very durable.
- The container is quite suitable for lightweight plastic construction toys, make-believe people and animals, or felt board images.
- Turn larger containers into waste paper baskets.
- Store multi-colored paper that will be used for gluing projects in the container.
- Use very small containers to hold paper clips.

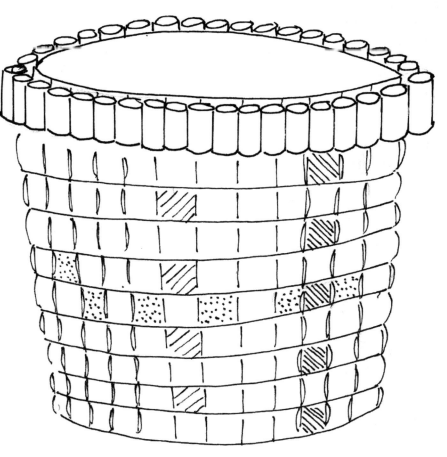

Rag Basket

Materials

Fabric or clothing
Thread and needle

How to Make

1. Tear fabric into 3" (7 cm) strips. Fold the strips into thirds.
2. Lay the strips next to each other to form the desired size.
3. Weave the strips in and out in the opposite direction until complete. Fold in half.
4. Stitch the sides together.
5. To create handles, braid lengths of fabric. Stitch the handles in place.

How to Use

- This woven rag basket is best if it is large. The knife crease base works best for standup storage purposes to hold a large volume of materials.
- Store extra towels or clothing in the basket.
- This basket is very lightweight—it's ready for the next field trip.

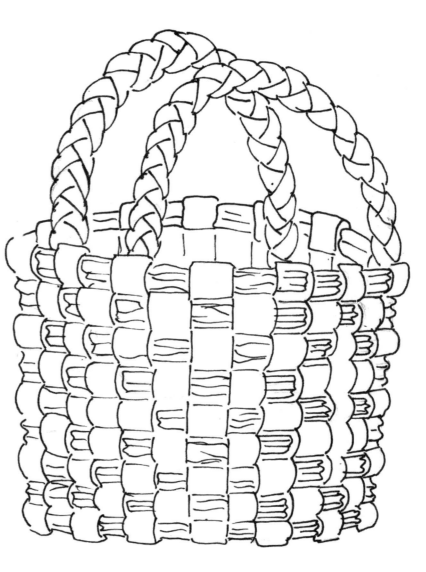

Cardboard Cube

Materials
Two-ply cardboard
Knife or saw
Carpenter's glue
Heavy object

How to Make
1. Determine how big the cube will be—a useful size is 12" x 12" (30 cm x 30 cm). Cut five squares of cardboard the determined size.
2. Apply glue to the edges of four squares and to the surface to which the edges will come in contact. Allow the glue to become tacky.
3. Place the cardboard pieces in position and weigh them down with a heavy object. Allow the glue to dry (up to two days) before attempting to attach the bottom.
4. Apply glue to the four bottom edges. Allow the glue to become tacky. Attach the bottom piece of cardboard to the edges.
5. Weigh it down with a heavy object. Allow the glue to dry and remove the object.

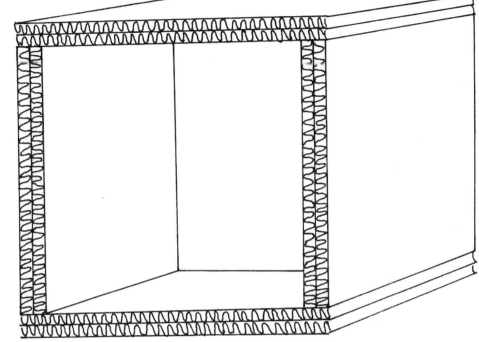

How to Use
- Cubes are versatile. Place them upright and use them as containers, or place them on their sides and use them as mini-storage units.
- A series of cubes placed on their sides, one on top of the other, becomes a series of nesting places for collections.
- Cubes are lightweight and easily manipulated by children. They offer children opportunities to engage in arranging and rearranging both the cube units and their contents. This can prove to be a joyous aesthetic experience.
- Cubes of various sizes and depths can be a satisfying alternative to plastic toy bins.
- Paint the cube or cover it with paper or fabric so it harmonizes with the classroom setting.

APPENDIX H

Nails

Nail Type	Size	'Penny Size'	Use
Common Nails	1 ¼"	3d	where the head is
	1 ½"	4d	not objectionable
	1 ¾"	5d	
	2"	6d	
	2 ¾"	7d	
Casing Nails	1 ½"	4d	on cabinets (cupboards) and trim
	2"	6d	counter-sink
	2 ½"	8d	cover with putty
	3"	10d	heavier than finishing nails
	3 ¼"	12d	
	3 ½"	16d	
	4"	20d	
Finishing Nail	1 ¼"	3d	round head
	1 ½"	4d	drive flush with the surface
	2"	6d	can also be counter-sunk
	2 ½"	8d	
Common Brads	Designated by size only		
	⅜"		thinner, smaller, and shorter
	½"		than finishing nails
	⅝"		used for light assembly
	¾"		
	1"		
	1 ¼"		
	1 ½"		

Anthropometric Chart for a Child-Scaled Environment[1]

Children's Dimensions Dimensions in Inches	Infants	Toddlers	Pre-School Age	School Age	
a. Crawling height	13 ¾	16	19 ½	21 ½	24 ½
b. Standing height	29	33 ¾	41	46	54 ¼
c. Eye level	25	30 ½	36 ½	41 ½	43 ¾
d. Overhead reach	38	44 ¼	49 ¼	53 ½	66
e. Seat height	20 [1]	7 ½	10	11	13
f. Table height (seated)	27 [1]	14	17 ½	18 ½	22
g. Eye level (seated)	33	25	29 ¼	34 ¼	37 ¼
h. Table height (standing)	—	17	20	24	29
i. Vertical reach between rungs	—	11 ½	16 ½	24 ¼	23
j. Rung diameter	[2]	1 ¼	1 ½	1 ¾	2 ¼
k. Stair rise	1–3	3	4	5	6
l. Slope	14°	14°	19°	25°	35°

1. Infant feeding chair seat height
2. No loose items in infant areas should be less than 1 ½" (4 cm) in diameter

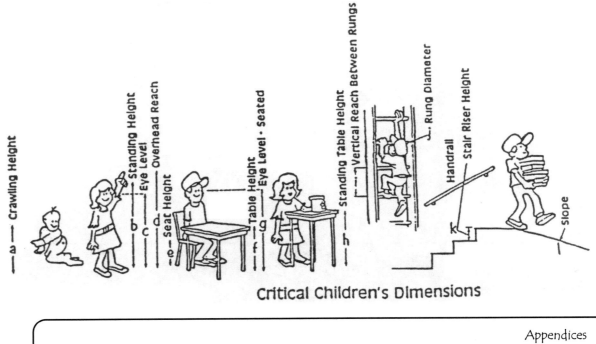

Critical Children's Dimensions

[1] From "Regulation 608-10" (p. 166), by the Department of the Army, Effective 12 March 1990, *Personal Affairs: Child Development Services*. Unclassified.

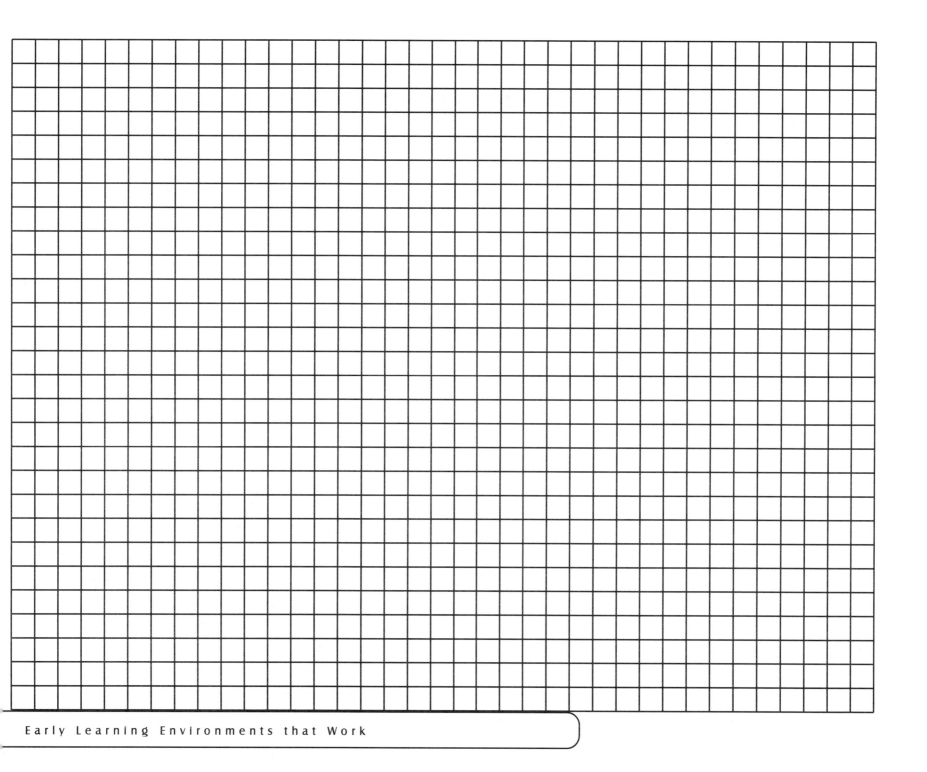

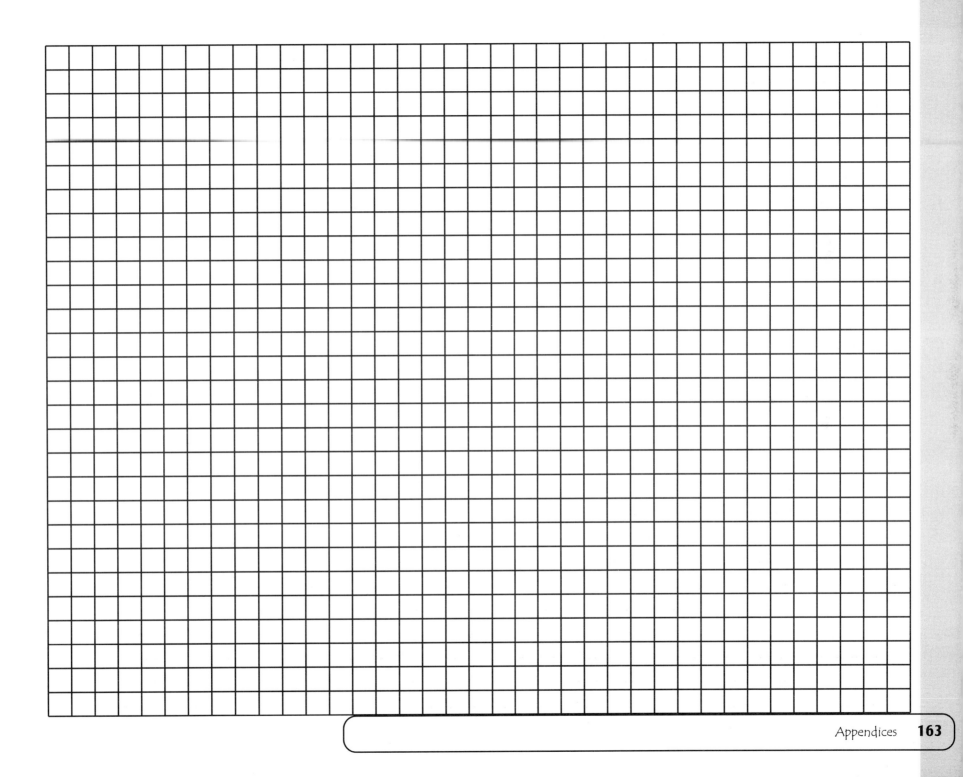

Appendix J

CENTERS

- Art Area
- Alternate Art Area
- Block Area
- Communication Area
- Dramatic Play Area
- Greeting Area
- Group Meeting Area
- Library Area
- Loft Area
- Music Area
- Science Area

Art Area

Alternate Art Area

Block Area

Communication Area

Dramatic Play Area

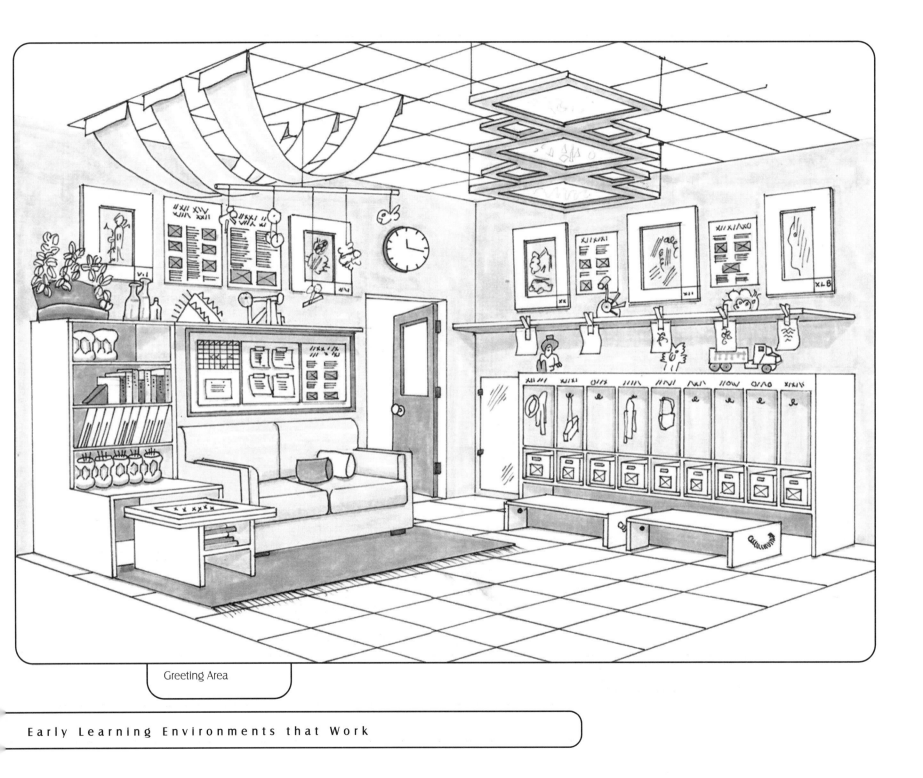

Greeting Area

Group Meeting Area

Library Area

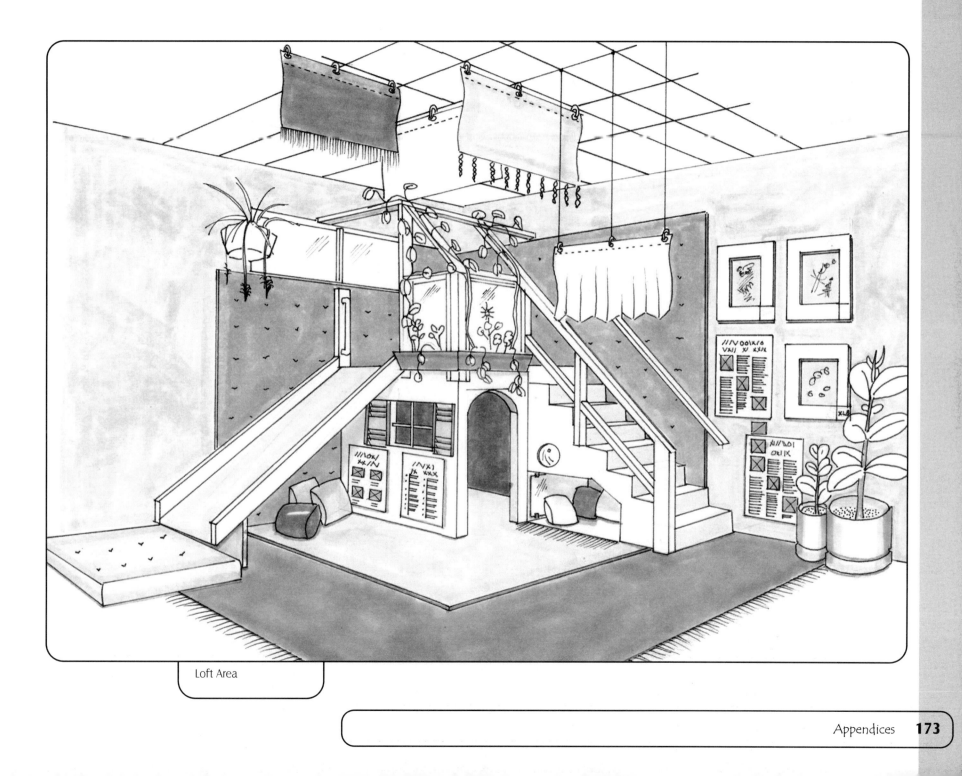

Loft Area

Music Area

Science Area

Index

Early Childhood Workshops That Work!

The Essential Guide to Successful Training and Workshops

Nancy P. Alexander

Make in-service training and workshops effective, interactive, and rewarding experiences! An effective early childhood workshop or in-service training session doesn't just happen. Good training results from the instructor's skill, knowledge, and ability to plan a session based on what participants need and want.

Early Childhood Workshops that Work! is a comprehensive guide that illustrates how to design, organize, conduct, and evaluate effective early childhood workshop and training seminars. It also includes sections on troubleshooting problem situations and designing learning materials. The author offers tips, guidance, and inside information from her years of experience as a successful workshop leader. 192 pages.

ISBN 978-0-87659-215-1 / Gryphon House / 13876 / Paperback

The Inclusive Early Childhood Classroom

Easy Ways to Adapt Learning Centers for All Children

Patti Gould and Joyce Sullivan

Written to help teachers look at classroom design in a new way, this book suggests ways of approaching activities so children with special needs can be successful. Each chapter focuses on either a learning center, such as art or science, or a time of the day, with particular attention to the child with special needs. 208 pages.

ISBN 978-0-87659-203-8 / Gryphon House / 19652 / Paperback

The Crisis Manual for Early Childhood Teachers

How to Handle the Really Difficult Problems

Karen Miller

The essential book to help you face those really difficult issues in the classroom. Learn effective strategies that address the most challenging problems you may encounter as a teacher, such as: the death of a family member, domestic violence, substance abuse, sexual abuse, homelessness, natural disasters, and children with HIV/AIDS. 384 pages.

ISBN 978-0-87659-176-5 / Gryphon House / 13748 / Paperback

The Portfolio Book

A Step-by-Step Guide for Teachers

Elizabeth F. Shores and Cathy Grace

The Portfolio Book introduces a method to help early childhood teachers improve the responsiveness of their teaching. The ten-step guide lets teachers begin to work with portfolio assessment at a comfortable pace. This book breaks the portfolio assessment process into small, easy-to-manage steps that can be integrated painlessly into everyday teaching. 192 pages.

ISBN 978-0-87659-194-9 / Gryphon House / 15468 / Paperback

The Complete Resource Book

An Early Childhood Curriculum, Over 2000 Activities and Ideas

Pam Schiller and Kay Hastings

The Complete Resource Book is an absolute must-have for every teacher. Offering a complete plan for every day of every week of the year, this is an excellent reference book for responding to children's specific interests. Each daily plan contains: circle time activities, music and movement activities, suggested books, and six learning center ideas. The appendix is jam-packed with songs, recipes, and games. 463 pages.

ISBN 978-0-87659-195-6 / Gryphon House / 15327 / Paperback

The Complete Learning Center Book

An Illustrated Guide for 32 Different Early Childhood Learning Centers

Rebecca Isbell

Enrich your classroom with unique learning centers and new ideas for traditional centers. Clear illustrations provide a layout of each center with suggestions for setting up the classroom environment. Each section includes an introduction, learning objectives, a letter to parents, related vocabulary, and a web of integrated learning that diagrams the range of curriculum areas taught. All you need to know about these 32 learning centers is included in this comprehensive book. 365 pages.

ISBN 978-0-87659-174-1 / Gryphon House / 17584 / Paperback

Transition Tips and Tricks

For Teachers

Jean Feldman

The author of the best-selling book *Transition Time* brings you more attention-grabbing, creative activities that provide children with an outlet for wiggles, while giving their brains a jump start with cross-lateral movement games. Capture their attention with songs, games, and fingerplays for any time of the day. These classroom-tested ideas are sure to become favorites! 216 pages.

ISBN 978-0-87659-216-8 / Gryphon House / 16728 / Paperback

Start Smart!

Building Brain Power in the Early Years

Pam Schiller

Did you know that emotions boost our memory? Or that small muscle exercises help the brain develop? Early experiences contribute to the future capacity of the brain. *Start Smart!* offers simple, straightforward ways to boost brain power with active exploration, repetition, sensory exploration, meaningful context, trial and error, and direct experience. All the activities are accompanied by explanations of how and why they help the brain develop. Easy and fun, *Start Smart!* will start young children ages three to six on their way to a future rich with learning! 192 pages.

ISBN 978-0-87659-201-4 / Gryphon House / 19378 / Paperback

The GIANT Encyclopedia of Theme Activities for Children 2 to 5

Over 600 Favorite Activities Created by Teachers for Teachers

Edited by Kathy Charner

This popular potpourri of over 600 classroom-tested activities actively engages children's imaginations and provides many months of learning fun. Organized into 48 popular themes, from Dinosaurs to Circuses to Outer Space, these favorites are the result of a nationwide competition. 511 pages.

ISBN 978-0-87659-166-6 / Gryphon House / 19216 / Paperback

The GIANT Encyclopedia of Circle Time and Group Activities for Children 3 to 6

Over 600 Favorite Circle Time Activities Created by Teachers for Teachers

Edited by Kathy Charner

Open to any page in this book and you will find an activity for circle or group time written by an experienced teacher. Filled with over 600 activities covering 48 themes, this book is jam-packed with ideas that were tested by teachers in the classroom. 510 pages.

ISBN 978-0-87659-181-9 / Gryphon House / 16413 / Paperback

The GIANT Encyclopedia of Art & Craft Activities for Children 3 to 6

More Than 500 Art & Craft Activities Written by Teachers for Teachers

Edited by Kathy Charner

Teacher-created, classroom-tested art activities to actively engage children's imaginations! The result of a nationwide competition, these art and craft activities are the best of the best. Just the thing to add pizzazz to your day! 568 pages.

ISBN 978-0-87659-209-0 / Gryphon House / 16854 / Paperback

The GIANT Encyclopedia of Science Activities for Children 3 to 6

Over 600 Favorite Science Activities Created by Teachers for Teachers

Edited by Kathy Charner

Leave your fears of science behind as our *GIANT Encyclopedia* authors have done. Respond to children's natural curiosity with over 600 teacher-created, classroom-tested activities guaranteed to teach your children about science while they are having fun. The result of a nationwide contest, *The GIANT Encyclopedia of Science Activities* joins our bestselling *GIANT Encyclopedia* series. 575 pages.

ISBN 978-0-87659-193-2 / Gryphon House / 18325 / Paperback